"If *Dark Souls* and *Elden Ring* deliver us ludic incomprehension, then Caracciolo delivers his customary analytical clarity. The book's replay value promises to attract both gamers and academics, keeping all of our intellectual health bars high."

David Ciccoricco, author of *Refiguring Minds in Narrative Media* and *Reading Network Fiction*

On Soulsring Worlds

The first book-length study devoted to FromSoftware games, *On Soulsring Worlds* explores how the *Dark Souls* series and *Elden Ring* are able to reconcile extreme difficulty in both gameplay and narrative with broad appeal.

Arguing that the games are strategically positioned in relation to contemporary audiences and designed to tap into the new forms of interpretation afforded by digital media, the author situates the games vis-à-vis a number of current debates, including the posthuman and the ethics of gameplay. The book delivers an object lesson on the value of narrative (and) complexity in digital play and in the interpretive practices it gives rise to.

Cross-fertilizing narrative theory, game studies, and nonhuman-oriented philosophy, this book will appeal to students and scholars of game studies, media studies, narratology, and video game ethnography.

Marco Caracciolo is Associate Professor of English and Literary Theory at Ghent University in Belgium. Drawing inspiration from cognitive science, the philosophy of mind, and the environmental humanities, his work explores the forms of experience afforded by narrative in literary fiction and video games. He is the author of several books, including most recently *Contemporary Narrative and the Spectrum of Materiality* (2023).

Routledge Advances in Game Studies

Immersion, Narrative, and Gender Crisis in Survival Horror Video Games
Andrei Nae

Videogames and the Gothic
Ewan Kirkland

Longing, Ruin, and Connection in Hideo Kojima's Death Stranding
Amy M. Green

Manifestations of Queerness in Video Games
Gaspard Pelurson

Representing Conflicts in Games
Antagonism, Rivalry, and Competition
Edited by Björn Sjöblom, Jonas Linderoth, and Anders Frank

Videogames and Agency
Bettina Bódi

Posthuman Gaming
Avatars, Gamers, and Entangled Subjectivities
Poppy Wilde

Traveling through Video Games
Tom van Nuenen

Metagames: Games about Games
Agata Waszkiewicz

On Soulsring Worlds
Narrative Complexity, Digital Communities, and Interpretation in *Dark Souls* and *Elden Ring*
Marco Caracciolo

For more information about this series, please visit: https://www.routledge.com/Routledge-Advances-in-Game-Studies/book-series/RAIGS

On Soulsring Worlds

Narrative Complexity, Digital Communities, and Interpretation in *Dark Souls* and *Elden Ring*

Marco Caracciolo

LONDON AND NEW YORK

First published 2024
by Routledge
4 Park Square, Milton Park, Abingdon, Oxon OX14 4RN

and by Routledge
605 Third Avenue, New York, NY 10158

Routledge is an imprint of the Taylor & Francis Group, an informa business

British Library Cataloguing-in-Publication Data
A catalogue record for this book is available from the British Library

Library of Congress Cataloging-in-Publication Data
Names: Caracciolo, Marco, author.
Title: On Soulsring Worlds : narrative complexity, digital communities, and interpretation in Dark Souls and Elden Ring / Marco Caracciolo.
Description: Abingdon, Oxon ; New York, NY : Routledge, 2024. | Series: Routledge advances in game studies | Includes bibliographical references and index.
Identifiers: LCCN 2023052313 (print) | LCCN 2023052314 (ebook) | ISBN 9781032683997 (hardback) | ISBN 9781032684017 (paperback) | ISBN 9781032684024 (ebook)
Subjects: LCSH: Video games--Design. | Dark souls (Video game) | Elden Ring (Video game) | Narration (Rhetoric)--Philosophy. | Video games--Moral and ethical aspects.
Classification: LCC GV1469.3 .C367 2024 (print) | LCC GV1469.3 (ebook) | DDC 794.8--dc23/eng/20231218
LC record available at https://lccn.loc.gov/2023052313
LC ebook record available at https://lccn.loc.gov/2023052314

ISBN: 978-1-032-68399-7 (hbk)
ISBN: 978-1-032-68401-7 (pbk)
ISBN: 978-1-032-68402-4 (ebk)

DOI: 10.4324/9781032684024

Typeset in Times New Roman
by Deanta Global Publishing Services, Chennai, India

Contents

Figures

Acknowledgments

This project is something of an outlier for me. Instead of writing a theory-first book, I decided to foreground a number of artifacts and listen to their resonances with theories I pursued in past work, from narratology to posthumanism. The artifacts in question are digital ones, four video games created by Japanese studio FromSoftware: the *Dark Souls* series (2011–16) and *Elden Ring* (2022). Like many others, I had no prior FromSoftware experience when *Elden Ring* was released in February 2022: despite struggling mightily with the first hours of the game, I was captivated, and ended up playing it for more time than I care to admit here. When I felt like I was hitting diminishing returns with *Elden Ring* (around my third playthrough), I went back to FromSoftware's earlier games and started making my way through them. Again, I was impressed with the sophistication of FromSoftware's creative vision, how each of the three *Dark Souls* games paves the way for *Elden Ring*'s open world while maintaining a distinctive identity and mood. Simultaneously, I was becoming increasingly familiar with the community of FromSoftware fans and with their internet-based practices of gameplay analysis and lore exposition. I found myself digging deeper and deeper into these debates, appreciating their liveliness and open-endedness—and the attention to detail that underlies many of them. While these practices are not exclusive to FromSoftware games, the depth and thoughtfulness of FromSoftware-related discussions stand out in the landscape of contemporary gaming. I was thus inspired to write a book about how *Dark Souls* games and *Elden Ring* can use intricate gameplay and narrative design to capture players' attention and cultivate complexity in online communities. The book focuses on six layers of this interplay of form and experience, starting from FromSoftware's approach to world building (temporality and spatiality) and ending with interpretation and ethics. In two middle chapters, I examine the games' understanding of humanness and community and how these ideas speak to some of the most pressing challenges of the present, from regulating online behavior to the disruption of Western dichotomies between human subjectivity and the nonhuman world.

I am, as always, thankful to the many colleagues and friends who listened to me talk about FromSoftware games, both formally and informally, and offered perceptive questions and stimulating feedback throughout the writing process. In late 2022, a workshop at the University of Oslo provided a first forum to share my ideas on Soulsring games (as I am calling *Dark Souls* and *Elden Ring* collectively). In 2023, I presented materials from this book at a symposium hosted by the University of Groningen on the subject of "Puzzling Stories" and at the annual conference of the International Society for the Study of Narrative in Dallas. Among those who generously engaged with my ideas on those occasions are Marco Bernini, Sarah Bro Trasmundi, Dave Ciccoricco, Melanie Kreitler, Karin Kukkonen, Cody Mejeur, Merja Polvinen, Dan Punday, David Rodriguez, Essi Varis, Steven Willemsen, and Sean Yeager. In Ghent, too, I had the opportunity to discuss FromSoftware games with Chris Chan, Ramses De Ruyck, Ciarán Kavanagh, and Alexander Vandewalle. I am grateful to my other collaborators—Simona Adinolfi, Shannon Lambert, Jonas Vanhove, and Hongri Wang—for accepting, seemingly without puzzlement, that my next project was going to involve a video game series they had never heard of. Finally, I would like to thank my partner, Wibke Schniedermann, for the comfort of our split-screen evenings, to which this book owes its existence.

A Note on Abbreviations and References

Throughout this book, I abbreviate *Dark Souls* as *DS* and *Elden Ring* as *ER*. I use the notes to provide URLs for Reddit posts, YouTube videos, and comments, as well as community-maintained websites (Fextralife, Fandom.com). All of these URLs are functional at the time of writing. References to scholarly or media sources (for which authorship can be straightforwardly established) are presented using the author-date system.

Introduction

As I was taking my first, shaky steps in the world of *Dark Souls*—a video game series developed by Japanese studio FromSoftware—the most immediate comparison that presented itself wasn't with other games I had played before but with the peculiar difficulties of modernist literature. Vicki Mahaffey describes these difficulties as follows:

> One of the main challenges of modernist writing in the twentieth century was to re-awaken in its audience a willingness to relinquish the self-satisfaction of easy accomplishment in favor of immersion in the flux, the seeming desolation, of what is left to know. The most immediate—if not the most popular—way of disrupting the illusion of knowing is by darkening or obscuring the textual surface. Stylistically, such obfuscation may serve to express the elusiveness and even the horror of reality; one could argue that it symbolically forces its readers to bear witness to the unspeakable incoherences and violent nonsense of the real.
>
> (Mahaffey 2007, 14)

For Mahaffey, works by Virginia Woolf, T. S. Eliot, and Samuel Beckett bombard readers with textual challenges that are a source of frustration but also of unique intellectual and ethical stimulation, at least if the reader is willing to put in the work. The difficulty can only be surmounted through patience and dedication, and it is central to the artistic vision and emotional effects of modernism.

Mahaffey's discussion of modernist literature finds unlikely echoes in Daniel Vella's reading of the first *Dark Souls* game: "the game's elevated kinaesthetic difficulty [prevents] the player from obtaining complete knowledge of its cosmos, … reflecting its concern with the mythical motif of the cursed Waste Land where sense and order has broken down" (Vella 2015). *Dark Souls* (2011) is the first of the three fantasy role-playing games developed by FromSoftware—largely under Hidetaka Miyazaki's creative direction, although Miyazaki was not directly involved in the development of *Dark Souls 2*. The desolate atmosphere of the *DS* series has a great deal in common

DOI: 10.4324/9781032684024-1

with the myth-infused, apocalyptic landscape of T. S. Eliot's seminal modernist poem *The Waste Land*, which is duly referenced by Vella's article on *DS1*. However, the parallels between modernist literature and Miyazaki's creation don't end there: both present the audience (readers or players) with a world that resists their attempts to know it fully; both use "obfuscation" as a tactic for entangling the player in ethical and existential questions that receive no clear answer. Moreover, just like modernist literature, *DS* games are startlingly hard to master. The idea of "relinquishing the self-satisfaction of easy accomplishment" describes with eerie precision the player's dismay when first faced with enemy encounters that seem infinitely more difficult than what most modern video games offer. In *DS* games, fights tend to require patient learning of the enemy's attack patterns, through loops of trial and error leading to gradual "immersion in the flux" (to quote again Mahaffey) of the combat.

Obviously, the differences between European modernism and FromSoftware games are at least as significant as their similarities: the difficulty of modernist art has been widely understood as an act of resistance against mass culture (see Pease 2011), while *DS* games, with their considerable following and millions of copies sold around the globe, are undoubtedly an expression of mass entertainment—and of Japanese gaming culture.[1] Perhaps most straightforwardly, the difficulty of modernist literature is interpretive, whereas the difficulty of *DS* is, as Vella acknowledges, primarily "kinaesthetic": it has its roots in game systems that reward speed and precision in interacting with the controls, as well as knowledge of game mechanics (such as a certain enemy's moves and weaknesses). In fact, this mechanical difficulty has played an important role in establishing FromSoftware's popularity as well as an entire video game genre—known as "souls-like" games—that mimics the arduous gameplay of the *DS* franchise.

Yet, it would be misleading to reduce *DS* and its two sequels (FromSoftware 2014, 2016) to their difficulty level. I am thinking here about the stereotypical association between FromSoftware games and the "rage quit" phenomenon immortalized by countless memes, whereby mounting frustration leads the player to abandon the game abruptly. There is much more to these games than kinesthetic difficulty resulting in smashed screens or controllers (a conventional byproduct of rage quitting). There is also more to these games than heated discussions surrounding difficulty and accessibility tend to suggest (see Harrison 2021). FromSoftware has refrained from including in its games the "easy mode" or accessibility options that can be found in many other video games, a design choice that has sparked extensive debates on social media. Some commentators argue that the ability to control the games' difficulty settings would result in a more diverse player base (including, for example, players with various forms of disability). Others, by contrast, suggest that difficulty is an integral part of the games' artistic vision, which would be greatly diminished if players could breeze through *DS* worlds.

Whatever side of that debate one falls on, the difficulty of *DS* games, while inextricable from the considerable skill they require, goes well beyond the mechanical challenges of gameplay. This is where the parallel with modernist literature does prove illuminating, because *DS* games immerse players in worlds that are at least as hard to decipher as the combat is hard to master. The same can be said about FromSoftware's latest offering, *Elden Ring* (2022), which reimagines *DS* on a larger canvas, affording a far more open experience than previous *DS* titles. The three *DS* games and *ER* refuse to hold the player's hand; instead, they craft a world that, while brimming with myth and history, appears remarkably reluctant to share its stories or introduce its systems. This reticence is another form of difficulty that FromSoftware audiences are asked to cope with, and it bears a striking resemblance to the interpretive challenges posed by modernist literature.

It is tempting, then, to understand FromSoftware games under the lens of Astrid Ensslin's (2014) concept of "literary gaming," by which she refers to digital games that present strategies commonly associated with literary works. Ensslin links literariness to the creative or unconventional use of verbal language in games: revisiting discussions on "defamiliarization" (Shklovsky 1965) or foregrounding (see, e.g., Miall and Kuiken 1994) in early twentieth-century literary theory, she identifies a range of linguistic experimentations in video games and interactive fiction. My discussion in this book stretches the concept of literary gaming even further: I argue that *DS* and *ER* are literary games not only because of the pressure they put on verbal language but also (and primarily) because they display remarkable complexity in gameplay, narrative, emotional, and ethical terms. As I will argue throughout, *DS* and *ER* don't spell anything out for the player's benefit but reward patience, attention to detail, and willingness to fill in narrative gaps, typically by taking numerous imaginative leaps. They thus call for a literary mode of engagement, which attaches value to their formal, thematic, and gameplay complexities.

Naturally, it is important to remember that FromSoftware games are games, not literary works: they are interactive artifacts that are enjoyed through gameplay and require an analytical toolbox that is considerably different from that of literary analysis. When I use phrases such as "literary engagement" or "complexity," I am not trying to impose a narrowly literary perspective on these games; rather, I am drawing an intermedial comparison to suggest the kind of complexity *DS* and *ER* are capable of. While my background is in literary studies and narrative theory, I draw ample inspiration from games research within the "ludological" tradition, which front-loads the study of game design.[2] I am particularly influenced by Ian Bogost's (2006) procedural criticism, which posits a close relationship between game mechanics and games' negotiation of ideological and cultural meanings.[3] Nevertheless, I also believe that theories and methods from literary studies can greatly enrich discussions on gaming, including discussions on topics such as narrative temporality, characterization, and ethics. Thus, this book builds on a broad array of sources in the hope of deepening the dialogue between games and literary scholarship.

FromSoftware is certainly not the only studio to craft games with a literary level of depth and sophistication. Especially in the space of "indie" gaming, one can find many such games.[4] *Outer Wilds* (Mobius Digital 2019), for example, or Lucas Pope's creations such as *Papers, Please* (2013) and *Return of the Obra Dinn* (2018) are also profoundly literary games: like FromSoftware's titles, they reward detailed exegesis of the kind historically found in literary scholarship, from nineteenth-century philology to the New Critics' "close reading" and their contemporary iterations.[5] But FromSoftware is no small indie studio, of course; it is one of the few major developers to combine an extremely wide appeal with literary complexity. As a result, a thriving community has emerged around FromSoftware games on social media platforms, and its engagements with the games tend to be as rich and sophisticated as the games themselves. One of this book's main themes is that attention to textual nuances is no longer limited to scholarship (literary or otherwise), but it defines the interpretive efforts of online communities, whose practices—as my approach to *DS* and *ER* fandom shows—often resemble scholarly discussion.

More generally, the book aims to demonstrate the value of closely reading the complex patterns traced by *DS* and *ER*, on multiple levels. I use the word "complex" to denote artifacts whose meaning is multisided, stratified, possibly self-contradictory, and difficult to uncover. This definition comes close to the etymology of complexity, a word that combines the Latin preposition "cum" (with) and the verb "plectere" (to weave or braid): things being folded or braided together. In my discussion of literary complexity, being woven together are multiple meanings, or levels of meaning, which can be recovered and pieced together only after close scrutiny. The concept of complexity can also be applied to cultural artifacts in a more specialized way, by drawing inspiration from the science of complex systems, which are characterized by properties such as emergence and self-organization.[6] However, the more informal use of the term is sufficient for my purposes here: a work (novel, game, etc.) is complex when it resists simple explanations and rewards multiple traversals, both literally (multiple playthroughs) and conceptually (multiple interpretations).[7] David Ciccoricco (2007) employs the term "complexity" in a very similar way to refer to the "cognitive workout" provided by Fumito Ueda's game *Shadow of the Colossus* (2005). Of course, I accept that different players and interpreters may arrive at different conclusions as to what counts as complex. When it comes to FromSoftware games, though, the number of players who seemingly regard them as complex (at least going by online discussions) is considerable. This broad consensus justifies my focus on *DS* and *ER*, but I will also pay attention to differences in how players understand and ascribe meaning to this complexity.

My hope is that emphasis on literary complexity can productively reframe the debate surrounding difficulty in *DS* and *ER*. The considerable challenge of gameplay is never an end in itself in FromSoftware games; rather, it is a means of situating the player within a wide gamut of thematic and narrative challenges. In *DS* and *ER*, more than in most other contemporary games, daunting gameplay resonates with, and amplifies, a polyphony of meanings, which I seek to illustrate in the following chapters. Online communities have been particularly receptive to that interplay of difficulty and complexity, as I illustrate through regular references to (and quotations from) Reddit, YouTube videos or comments, and websites dedicated to *DS* and *ER*. This book isn't based on ethnographic work or data collection in any systematic sense, but my analysis is conducted in dialogue with players whose commentaries can be found online.[8] I have tried to clearly differentiate my autoethnographic observations from ideas I derived from the community, but I am also interested in exploring their areas of overlap or at least convergence: these commonalities help me demonstrate that *DS* and *ER* aren't only extremely complex games in themselves but that their complexity is matched by the sophistication and self-awareness of internet commentaries.

My discussion in this book distinguishes between six layers of complexity, but it is important to note that the layers aren't meant to be exhaustive and that my subdivision is primarily heuristic, since in *DS* and *ER* gameplay these dimensions tend to work in tandem. Before turning to an overview of the six layers (which organize the following chapters), it is worth commenting on the portmanteau word Soulsring in this book's title. This is the shorthand I will use throughout for *DS* games and *ER* considered together. This neologism is inspired by the term Soulsborne, which is widely used on the internet to refer to two FromSoftware titles in addition to *DS* games: *Demon's Souls* (FromSoftware 2009) and *Bloodborne* (FromSoftware 2015). These are broadly reminiscent of *DS* in terms of gameplay. However, the basic formula of FromSoftware games has evolved significantly since the release of *Demon's Souls* (arguably, the archetype of all souls-like games). While *Demon's Souls* asks players to move back and forth between a number of relatively linear and completely independent worlds, *DS* games and *ER* are set within a single, highly interconnected world. *DS1* was the first FromSoftware game to popularize this intricate spatial design, which has become one of the hallmarks of what I call Soulsring games. Likewise, *Bloodborne* differs considerably in genre and setting from *DS* and *ER*: instead of these games' medieval fantasy, its Victorian-era setting has drawn comparisons with H. P. Lovecraft's fiction. The *Soulsborne* label is sometimes extended to *Sekiro: Shadows Die Twice* (FromSoftware 2019), which is another action game taking place in a fictionalized version of early modern Japan, with some recognizable *DS* features but also a substantially different, rhythm-based gameplay style.

These differences make the Soulsborne category too broad and diverse for the detailed analysis I aim to carry out in this book. Instead, I will limit my investigation to the three *DS* games (including their expansions or downloadable content [DLC]) and the more recent *ER*—Soulsring games, as I will refer to them collectively. This is a more manageable corpus but still reveals some significant trends in the evolution of FromSoftware games, particularly the cyclicity of plot across the three *DS* games and the considerably vaster and more open world of *ER*. In other respects, however, *DS* games and *ER* share a medieval fantasy setting and also some basic parameters of world building and what game fans and scholars refer to as "lore": that is, the backstories of the game world and its characters, seen as a collective archive.[9] Indeed, an important subgroup of the Soulsring community is engaged in the recovery and discussion of the games' lore, in a process that—given the terseness of much Soulsring storytelling—tends to blur the distinction between the exposition of an existing narrative and fan fiction. I will have much more to say about these practices, adopting the term "archaeological fandom" to describe the type of attention that many fans devote to the stratification of locations and (back)stories in the games, which is of course closely related to the stratification of meanings I express under the heading of literary complexity.

Six Layers of Complexity

The book starts by establishing the basic coordinates of Soulsring worlds, with chapters devoted to time and space that are intended to familiarize readers (including readers new to gaming) with the salient features and mechanics of FromSoftware games. Thus, I start with two chapters that understand complexity in formal terms, as a matter of game and narrative design, looking at how time and space are configured in *DS* and *ER*. In the chapters that follow, I tease out four more layers of complexity, whereby a stratification of meanings, while still grounded in formal structures and devices, emerges in the discussion of particular themes or concerns articulated by Soulsring games. These layers include the redrawing of the boundary of "humanity" to accommodate posthumanist insights (chapter 3); the particular type of community building afforded by Soulsring games through multiplayer cooperation (chapter 4); the self-awareness of online interpretations of the games' significance and personal relevance (chapter 5); and—last but not least—their negotiation of ethical difficulties (chapter 6).

Here is a more detailed overview of the chapters. Chapter 1 unpacks the games' nonlinear temporality by adopting the cognitive-linguistic concept of "image schema": simply put, I argue that any deviation from the schema of path-like movement will register in audiences as a form of nonlinearity. Soulsring games, however, combine multiple nonlinear schemata, which the chapter examines in detail: these include the loop of the player-character's constant death-and-rebirth cycles, the entanglement of the side quests, and the stratification of the game worlds' histories. Chapter 2 moves from time to space as a centerpiece of Soulsring games' complexity. Building on and expanding Henry Jenkins's (2004) influential concept of "environmental storytelling," the chapter examines how place becomes a blueprint for story in Soulsring games through evocative locations and item descriptions that deepen the player's engagement with the narrative. However, these spatial stories also leave numerous gaps and discontinuities in the player's experience that call for creative integration while resonating with the puzzling instability of the setting.

Chapter 3 shows that, like time and space, the concept of humanity that is implicated in Soulsring games also fluctuates widely. Despite featuring an anthropomorphic protagonist, these games depart from fantasy conventions in that they don't explicitly divide up their inhabitants into humans and nonhumans. Instead, the player is asked to work toward a radically open understanding of humanness that resonates with the posthumanist theories developed by Donna Haraway (2015) and Deborah Bird Rose (2011). After examining the peculiar mechanics that surround an item named "humanity" in *DS1*, I focus on the grotesque and metamorphosis as recurrent Soulsring motifs that embed the human within a network of nonhuman agents and forces.

Chapter 4 examines Soulsring games' unique approach to multiplayer experience through the lens of two concepts: asynchronous multiplayer and constrained communication. I show how less is more in the world of Soulsring games: paradoxically, the more limited and convoluted the games' multiplayer systems are, the more emotionally resonant the rare moments of interpersonal sharing become. Based on a Reddit survey, I argue that the mechanics implemented by FromSoftware foster community building in ways that depart from the shallowness and toxicity often associated with mainstream gaming culture.

The word "hermeneutics" triggers associations with nineteenth-century philology, not with Reddit discussions. Yet, as I argue in chapter 5, Soulsring games give rise to surprisingly sophisticated and self-conscious interpretive practices in online communities. Through close examination of Soulsring subreddits, YouTube videos, and the comments section on specialized websites, I offer a comprehensive account of how players negotiate the meanings of Soulsring games—that is, how they work through interpretive tensions and disagreements and how they connect the game worlds to personal experience, particularly (in a surprising number of online commentaries) mental health crises.

The final chapter turns to the ethical dimension of Soulsring games. Prima facie, their plot builds on a simple, even dichotomous moral universe. The symbolism of fire and darkness in *DS* plays into a long history of associating fire and light with morally worthy behavior, darkness with evil schemes. Yet, Soulsring games consistently disrupt ethical meaning making, by implicating players in the minor and major tragedies of the side quests or by asking them to choose between endings whose moral significance remains uncertain. In the final part of the chapter, I examine the recurring trope of the "poison swamp" and argue that it serves as an embodied allegory of the ethical difficulties staged by Soulsring games. Ultimately, I suggest that engagement with ethics might be the most promising way of articulating the complexity of Soulsring games and of valuing their signature difficulty.

Notes

1 I will not be able to discuss the Japanese roots of FromSoftware's works in this book, but many aspects of their game worlds are clearly influenced by Buddhist notions, perhaps starting from the cyclicity of the gameplay loop (see chapter 1). See Consalvo (2022) on the construction of "Japaneseness" in games designed for a global audience.
2 For more on ludology, see important early interventions by Markku Eskelinen (2001) and Gonzalo Frasca (2003a). Their publications helped shape the field of game studies, frequently in polemical opposition to scholars such as Henry Jenkins (2004) and Marie-Laure Ryan (2001), whose work was perceived by ludologists as more aligned with literary studies and the field of narratology in particular. I will return to this debate in chapter 2.
3 See also Murray (2017) for a more recent, cultural studies-inspired approach to the ideological relevance of video games.
4 On the aesthetics of indie gaming, see Juul's (2019) discussion.
5 For more on the history of philology, see Daston and Most (2015). See Smith (2016) for a relatively recent reappraisal of close reading.
6 See, e.g., John Pier's (2017) account of narrative as a complex system, and my own discussion in Caracciolo (2021, chap. 1). For more on complexity and (literary) narrative, see the collection edited by Grishakova and Poulaki (2019). I will have more to say about complexity in chapter 1.
7 The concept of "performative multiplicity" introduced by Jayemanne (2017) comes close to this account of complexity. For Jayemanne, performative multiplicity is key to understanding how games reward multiple engagements. Complex or literary games, in my terminology, seek to maximize the range of performances they offer on a gameplay, narrative, and interpretive level.
8 See the handbook by Boellstorff et al. (2013) for more on the ethnographic study of online gaming communities.
9 See also Tanya Krzywinska's (2008) definition and discussion of lore.

1 Complicating the Flow of Time

Early on in *DS1*, the player is told that the "flow of time itself is convoluted, with heroes centuries old phasing in and out. The very fabric wavers, and relations shift and obscure." The convoluted nature of time in Soulsring games explains why it is so difficult for the lore community to paint a definitive picture of the history of these game worlds. In a post on Reddit, dylanalduin writes about the discontinuities in the plot of *DS1* and *DS3*. Referring to one of *DS1*'s most beloved (and challenging) boss encounters, the Ornstein and Smough duo, this user asks: "If we killed Ornstein in *DS1*, how is he able to follow the Nameless King in *DS3*? How was Smough alive to defend the Cathedral?" For dylanalduin (who also quotes the passage about the convoluted flow of time), the answer is that the three *DS* games actually take place in parallel worlds and that their timelines can never be brought into complete alignment. This difficulty, dylanalduin acknowledges, "has created several problems for the lore-hunting community with continuity."[1] Soulsring games repeatedly encourage us to establish a timeline encompassing both the remote past of the worlds we explore and the intersecting narratives of the characters we encounter. Yet our attempts are constantly frustrated: if to relate means both to narrate and to link disparate things or events, many "relations" in these games remain, as *DS1* spells out with remarkable self-awareness, "obscure."

The inability to fully extrapolate the narrative of Soulsring games is a sign of their literary complexity: the opacity of their chronologies doesn't result in disengagement but rather feeds the player's interest in the abiding mystery of these games. Narrative-minded players are encouraged to fill in the gaps, coming up with lore theories and speculative answers to the many questions the games raise. They also debate their interpretations in online settings, building a body of collective knowledge but also negotiating differences in the meanings they ascribe to the Soulsring universe (see chapter 5). Of course, not all players will attach the same value to Soulsring narrativity—to use a narratological concept denoting the textual elements that call for narrative-based comprehension (Abbott 2014). Instead, some players will focus on the challenges of gameplay or on the visual attractions of the setting. But whether narrativity takes center stage in the player's experience or not, the nonlinear form of Soulsring games affords an opportunity for what I will

DOI: 10.4324/9781032684024-2

call an "archaeological" mode of engagement—that is, for attention to detail and appreciation of stratified meanings. This stance is closely related to the literary complexity I discussed in the introduction. What I will describe in this chapter as "shadowtime" or—alternatively—a "layering" or "percolation" of temporal planes is my entry point into complexity and the archaeological mindset that goes with it.

The topic of temporality has received some attention in game studies, most significantly in work by Jesper Juul (2005), Darshana Jayemanne (2017), and Christopher Hanson (2018). Juul tends to focus on the temporality of gameplay experience rather than on the temporal complexity inherent in a game's narrative cues. Juul draws a preliminary distinction between "play time" and "event time": the former denotes the temporality experienced by the player while engaging with the game, whereas the latter refers to the temporality traced by in-game events (for instance, a certain enemy is killed or a civilization reaches a new era in a strategy game). As typical of first-wave scholarship on games, Juul's account overlooks the way in which game narrative can complicate and diversify event time: while Juul hints at a possible parallel between the play versus event time distinction and Seymour Chatman's (1978) story versus discourse, he does not pursue the analogy. Instead, game time remains a relatively monolithic concept and falls short of addressing how multiple temporalities can be combined within a game's diegesis.

Hanson's discussion is more attuned to "the numerous temporalities found in video games" (2018, 11) but again downplays the role of storytelling in producing this multiplicity. (The words "narrative" and "story" are not even featured in the index, which is rather shocking for a book on temporality.) Instead, Hanson's argument foregrounds game mechanics that enable the direct manipulation of temporality (for instance, pausing or the save function in games) as well as the effects of immediacy that they create. Certainly, Hansen's insight that "many digital games and even entire genres emphasize repetition and mastery" (2018, 135) serves as an apt description of Soulsring games, but the ubiquity of repetitive loops is only a starting point if one wants to understand the convoluted form of time in these games.

More promising is Darshana Jayemanne's concept of "chronotypology," an analytical method that focuses on how games orchestrate multiple performances or traversals of the game world. Jayemanne's interest in multiplicity is broadly consistent with the idea, discussed in my introduction, that complexity in games rewards a range of gameplay and interpretive efforts. In contrast to both Juul and Hansen, Jayemanne acknowledges that narrative plays a key role in this orchestration of multiplicity and that this orchestration has both temporal and spatial dimensions. In relation to temporality specifically, Jayemanne adds that chronotypology allows game studies to move beyond a conventional binary of linear narrative and nonlinear gameplay (2017, 282). Soulsring games resonate with this approach; they disrupt the "flow of time" by challenging a linear understanding of narrative temporality. This disruption originates at the level of "event time," with the narrative cues preventing players from forming a coherent image of the games' timeline, but carries over to the experienced temporality of gameplay as well.

In general, narrative linearity can be defined as the path-like progression from one state of affairs to another. A certain event causes another event, which then causes a third event, and so on: these sequential chains of cause and effect are at the heart of linear storytelling. Typically, the causal chain is tied to the goals and desires of a character or protagonist: a character wants to save the world, or find love, or avenge their family, and the plot flows linearly from this goal. Most plots throw complications or obstacles in the way of the protagonist's goals: nevertheless, the audience remains aware of these goals; the more difficulties the character faces in realizing these goals, the more the teleology of the character's desires orients the audience's engagement with the character and thus the overall interpretation of the narrative.[2]

In video games, of course, the player has an active role in determining and pursuing the character's goals. We make choices, which—as game scholars have long recognized—tend to take the form of diverging paths. Marie-Laure Ryan (2006, 105–6), for example, distinguishes between three types of "interactive architectures affecting story": the tree, the flowchart, and the maze. In the tree type, every branching point is a decision moment; each branch splits into two or more branches, resulting in an increasingly vast structure where the branches never intersect. In the flowchart model, by contrast, the branches periodically converge, which limits the complexity of the structure and funnels the player's decisions into a handful of possible outcomes. The maze is a special case in that it doesn't map choices but the player's traversal of a game space: here the player doesn't primarily decide what happens in the game world, but where to go and what to see, with the story (as the outcome of the exploration) resulting from the locations the player has visited.

All these are multilinear structures in that the player is presented with a range of options and can determine the course of the narrative. But multilinearity is not necessarily the same as nonlinearity: even when multiple paths are available, our traversal of these paths can still trace (and generally does trace) a linear movement, from point A to point B. Thus, even if Ryan's maze diagram looks "convoluted" when viewed from this top-down perspective, from the perspective of a player making their way through a game, a sense of clear sequentiality may persist: as they define and pursue the protagonist's goals, players may have limited awareness of the overall structure of the game and instead focus on the step-by-step nature of their interactions. To put this point otherwise, the availability of decision making in games is no guarantee of nonlinearity. For nonlinearity to emerge in players' experience, games need to sever or destabilize the link between the player's actions, the goals they ascribe to the characters (particularly the player-controlled character), and the overall narrative structure.

How do Soulsring games complicate the "flow of time," then? Multiple gameplay mechanics and design choices help create this challenge to linearity, as I will discuss in this chapter. These range from the basic gameplay loop to asynchronous multiplayer (see chapter 4) and a number of narrative strategies implemented, in different ways, by the games. Before discussing and illustrating these devices, I will draw on scholarship on complex narrative in film. This work provides helpful contextualization for my analysis and also highlights the concept (derived from cognitive linguistics) of "image schema," which is key to understanding how game narratives—and Soulsring games in particular—put pressure on linearity. In the course of this discussion, I will also develop a distinction between two types of narrative complexity: puzzle-like complexity, in which linearity is challenged but the narrative can still be pieced together in a more or less systematic, chronological fashion; and real mystery complexity, in which nonlinearity raises a more sustained challenge to the player's ability to work out a chronology.

Focus on Complex Narratives

The idea of complexity in film or TV narrative is frequently linked to the temporal progression of plot. Thus, film scholars Steven Willemsen and Miklós Kiss write that fictional "stories frequently feature complex temporal structures that are radically different from our everyday—more or less linear—conception of time" (2020, 173). In film studies, narrative complexity is discussed under many headings, from "forking-path" (Bordwell 2002) and "network" narrative (Bordwell 2008) to "puzzle" (Buckland 2009b) and "mind-game" (Elsaesser 2009) films. These labels aren't always interchangeable, and they highlight different aspects or effects of complexity, but they reflect a shared interest in how film can complicate the flow of narrative time, particularly the expectation of a linear, sequential arrangement of events. Warren Buckland puts it succinctly: "A puzzle plot is intricate in the sense that the arrangement of events is not just complex, but complicated and perplexing; the events are not simply interwoven, but *entangled*" (2009a, 3).

Film audiences can of course always expect some degree of complication. Take for example flashbacks and flashforwards: these "anachronies," in Gérard Genette's (1980, 35–6) terminology, are at least as old as Homer, and a fairly common device in film and other narrative media. When engaging in anachronies, the storyteller typically facilitates the audience's task of reconstructing a chronological, linear sequence, for instance, by clearly signposting the shifts in time and keeping them manageable in number and scope. However, as the frequency of anachronies increases in a narrative, the structure can give rise to an experience of complexity and also to confusion or disorientation for audience members who struggle to keep track of the chronology. Christopher Nolan's film *Memento* (2000) has become a poster child for this type of complexity in contemporary film. The film, to use Buckland's metaphor, entangles black-and-white and color sequences. The former are shown in the correct (chronological) order, but they are periodically interrupted by color flashforwards, which are displayed in reverse order, from the end of the story to its beginning. The result is a deeply puzzling structure for the first-time viewer of the film, who has to put in considerable work to reconstruct the chronology—an operation that frequently involves rewatching or at least looking up a plot summary on the internet.

Anachronies are not the only device through which audiovisual narrative can create complexity, however. Time loop or time travel narratives build on temporal paradoxes: in the TV series *Russian Doll* (Lyonne, Headland, and Poehler 2019), for instance, the protagonist is returned to the same situation, on the same night, every time she dies. This is no simple flashback, because the protagonist remembers what happened in previous iterations of the loop, and also the world around her keeps changing slightly every time she dies.[3] But if the time loop structure of *Russian Doll* remains fairly accessible, a more experimental time travel narrative like Shane Carruth's film *Primer* (2004) increases narrative complexity significantly, presenting multiple versions of the same characters, and so on.

Kiss and Willemsen (2017; Willemsen and Kiss 2020) offer a discussion of narrative complexity in terms of the viewer's cognitive operations when faced with films such as *Memento* or *Primer*. Drawing inspiration from cognitive metaphor theory in George Lakoff and Mark Johnson's (1980) tradition, they argue that our understanding of time, including narrative time, is based on a number of image schemata, which are structures derived from everyday perception.[4] Through image schemata, we understand abstract concepts by mapping them onto physical structures or spatial relations (e.g., containment or superimposition). Movement along a path is one of such structures, and it can be used to conceptualize abstract phenomena through a metaphorical operation: for instance, when I talk about a presidential candidate's "path to victory," I am not talking about the candidate's physical movement, but rather metaphorically referring to something more abstract—namely, the strategies they must implement to achieve success.

The schema of movement along a path is also frequently used to describe the passage of time ("we are getting closer to Christmas"), and in fact, the idea of narrative linearity itself presupposes a conceptual analogy between the organization of narrative time and the path schema. We understand narrative by mapping the events onto a path-like structure or vector oriented, as we have seen, by the protagonist's goals and desires. This is not necessarily a conscious operation: most of the time, the mapping takes place automatically as part of narrative comprehension. As Kiss and Willemsen (2017; Willemsen and Kiss 2020) argue based on work in psycholinguistics, this mapping facilitates the audience's understanding of narrative sequentiality and causality. The easier it is to apply a path mental schema, the more linear the narrative we are engaging with will appear.

In narrative, path-like structures can be evoked in a number of ways. One of them is physical movement (such as a journey), but this movement is typically accompanied by a more psychological kind of tension: a character moves through space to realize a certain goal. Thus, the path-like structure of linearity is often associated in narrative with teleological orientation—the tendency to closely follow a character's desires and goals, which serve as a vector in linear progression. Narrative complexity—for instance, in the case of *Memento*—prevents audiences from straightforwardly applying the path schema. This doesn't mean that the path will play no role in narrative comprehension: in fact, as the audience struggles to establish chronological sequencing, they will attempt to arrange the events onto a path-like structure. But as they do so, other image schemata will become implicated in narrative comprehension: for instance, Willemsen and Kiss (2020, 186) analyze the plot of *Inception* (another film by Christopher Nolan) in terms of the spatial schemata of containment and verticality. Containment suggests the embedding of narrative layers in the film, whereas verticality captures a hierarchy, with "the film's reality forming the top level and each additional dream-level below that providing an understanding of these timelines as 'deeper' layers into which the characters 'descend'" (2020, 187). By applying these schemata, viewers retain some degree of cognitive control over the narrative of *Inception*, although the process is far more complicated and uncertain than when we simply build on the path schema. In other cases of narrative complexity, schemata related to circularity (such as cycle) might come into play as well: time loop narratives are an excellent example of this. Put otherwise, in complex narrative the path schema for time will be challenged by other mental patterns that *don't* denote unidirectional movement in space. The audience's understanding of narrative time is still grounded in schemata derived from bodily experience, but the path schema—which is conventionally associated with narrative—doesn't fit; instead, alternative schemata become implicated in narrative comprehension.

Nevertheless, complex narratives differ widely in terms of how fully they can be understood through schemata other than path. If we see these narratives as "puzzles," to quote again Buckland, then that metaphor strongly hints at the possibility of a solution to the puzzle: the narratives—no matter how much pressure they put on the path schema—can be fully explicated by resorting to patterns such as containment or cycle. To return to the *Memento* example, this is a puzzle film in the literal sense that the chronology can be pieced together in a way that leaves very little room for mystery or ambiguity. In image-schematic terms, one could say that *Memento* uses patterns such as entanglement and backward movement to organize (and complicate) its presentation of a relatively straightforward story. When and if the audience identifies the correct schemata with which to interpret the narrative (and this, as I mentioned, may be an unconscious process), the puzzle is cracked once and for all. Other complex narratives, by contrast, disrupt the path schema—that is, narrative linearity—but an alternative image-schematic understanding of the story (a "solution" to the puzzle) doesn't crystallize: instead, events or plot lines are left dangling, ambiguously and (for some audience members) frustratingly. This is an effect associated with the arthouse cinema of, for example, David Lynch (see Kiss and Willemsen 2017, chap. 5), which frequently doesn't provide enough information to fully reconstruct a chronology—or disrupts path-like progression to such an extent that most audience members will give up their attempts to find a solution.

Narrative complexity thus occupies a broad spectrum that goes from the "puzzle" (in which the chronology can be worked out fully) to what I will call, following Porter Abbott (2013), a "real mystery" (that is, one that remains riddled with uncertainty). Across this spectrum, linearity is disrupted and the audience reaches for alternative image schemata to make sense of a set of narrative cues. But while in the puzzle the image schemata facilitate narrative comprehension, in real mysteries these schemata become implicated in the audience's experience without fully illuminating the progression of narrative. We will see at the end of this chapter that Soulsring games are strongly aligned with real mystery complexity. Path-like linearity is consistently undermined, and the cycle as an image schema proves helpful to understand certain gameplay and narrative elements. Entanglement and superimposition are two further image-schematic structures active in our engagement with the games' quest lines and multiple temporal planes. However, even those patterns don't offer a fully satisfying solution to the questions raised by the games. This setup creates the "continuity problems" noted by Reddit user dylanalduin, but it also fosters the avid engagement with Soulsring narratives that can be observed in online communities. In the next section, I will tease out the gameplay elements that complicate linear image schemata in the player's Soulsring experience, moving from the loop created by the games' inherent difficulty to the entanglement of main and secondary quests, and finally discussing the stratification of temporal planes.

The Gameplay Loop

I have already mentioned that dying is an integral part of the Soulsring experience: even the most skilled and experienced players will die countless times in the course of a playthrough. *DS2* features an in-game death count, which is shown on a monument near the game's main hub (the Firelink Shrine): if the game is started in online mode, this monument records the number of times players have died worldwide—in 2018, four years after the game's release, this figure was already above 300 million.[5] If one is playing offline, by contrast, the monument shows how many times the player has died (for me, this was over 500 times after playing the game for around 50 hours). Dying is of course a common event in many if not most video games: but perhaps more than any other game, Soulsring games ask the player to become comfortable with repeated deaths.[6] This is because of the game's difficulty level, which is compounded by the fact that every death results in significant loss of progress. Typically, the player will arrive in a new location and find a save point (known as a bonfire in *DS*, site of grace in *ER*). From that point onward, the enemies waylaying the player will respawn (that is, come back to life) as soon as the player dies: only bosses and minibosses—powerful, unique creatures—do not respawn after death. Thus, in most areas, with every death players are returned to the latest save point, where they are asked to take on the same enemies in an attempt to make it to the next bonfire or site of grace. But while it may look like we are starting from scratch every time, in fact every death is an opportunity to learn something new about our surroundings and the enemies we are facing: Soulsring areas are rich in shortcuts, so forming a mental map of every level is key to the player's survival (as discussed in the next chapter). Awareness of enemy placement and familiarity with the weaknesses and attack patterns of various enemy types are also essential lessons we can learn with each playthrough of a certain area. At a basic level, then, Soulsring gameplay is organized according to the image schema of a loop, where the loop indicates repetition with (the possibility of) difference: while seemingly returning us to square one, every death can teach us something about the game world. This basic pattern is of course something that Soulsring games share with many other games, and in fact, the time loop form in TV series and film can be viewed as a reference to or remediation of video game experience.[7] But the sheer number of death cycles in these games inevitably foregrounds the loop schema in the player's imagination and disrupts the ease of linear progress.

"You Will Walk Those Grounds without Really Knowing Why": The Main Quest

Despite the insistence on the loop, Soulsring games cue the possibility of path-like progression. At the start of each game, we are assigned what may look like a "quest," which is a prototypical instance of linear narrative: the protagonist, the player-character, has a certain goal—namely, "linking the fire" in *DS* games or restoring the Elden Ring after the Shattering.[8] This goal orients our interactions with the game teleologically, by creating a path-like structure for us to follow. In *ER*, the in-game map even shows "guidance of grace" icons that point the player in the right direction for advancing the main story. Grace is a metaphysical force in the world of the game, emanating from the Erdtree (a giant tree visible in the distance) and thus indirectly from the divine Golden Order. On a gameplay level, the guidance of grace is needed in *ER* because the open-world structure of the game places fewer constraints on the player's movement than in the more focused level design of *DS* games: by following the signposting of grace, the player is put on a relatively linear trajectory—although they may always decide to ignore the guidance.

Further, the recipe of all Soulsring games evokes a highly linear narrative template, something like a rags-to-riches story in which a lowly character (the "chosen undead" [*DS1*], "bearer of the curse" [*DS2*], "ashen one" [*DS3*], or "tarnished" creature [*ER*]) acquires new powers and takes on increasingly challenging enemies. This is a setup reminiscent of Joseph Campbell's (1949) influential "hero's journey," which is another linear structure implicated in the player's understanding of the game world.

Still, even as the games repeatedly hint at path-like progression, the linearity of the player's quest is constantly destabilized. The loop schema of the player's death cycles represents a first step in this direction, but Soulsring games deploy much more sophisticated strategies to keep players from sticking to the path schema too closely. To remain at the level of the framing of the player's "quest": I have mentioned the player's goals, but it should be noted that a great deal of murkiness surrounds the action of restoring the fire or the Elden Ring. As YouTuber VaatiVidya remarks in a video essay on the plot of *DS2*, the game foregrounds the theme of desire ("want") but also pointedly refrains from revealing the main characters' goals: "[Their] wants are hidden from us until the very end."[9] This uncertainty of desire extends to the player-character's own quest: at the start of the game, we are told that in order to dispel the "undead curse" that afflicts this land, the player must take the throne in Castle Drangleic (named, appropriately enough, Throne of Want) and become the new king. This seems clear enough at first, but on closer look, the reason why realizing this goal would end the curse remains shrouded in mystery, as the theories and interpretations that circulate on *DS* subreddits attest.[10] Partly, this is due to the fact that for most of the game we only get snippets of information on the curse and our own quest, from multiple characters who represent different and frequently conflicting perspectives on the game world. The mystery of the curse is further compounded by its embedding within the larger *DS* mythos of the Age of Fire: the primeval fire is almost extinguished, and the player (in all *DS* games) can decide to either keep it alive, thus extending the Age of Fire, or let it go out and usher in a new Age of Dark. In the video essay mentioned above, VaatiVidya suggests that the undead curse hits every time the First Flame is about to die, as a prefiguration of impending catastrophe, but this is an extrapolation that the game never fully ratifies. As VaatiVidya also notes, the previous king of Drangleic, Vendrick, appeared to ignore or misunderstand the link between the curse and the Age of Fire: in that respect, the king is in the dark, not unlike the player who is tasked to replace him.

Indirectly, then, the quest to end the curse in *DS2* puts us on a path toward the First Flame (where fire originated in *DS* mythology). After defeating the game's final boss, the player-character can either "link the flame," sacrificing themselves to ensure the continuation of the Age of Fire or walk away and become Dark Lord. This is a reenactment of the ending of *DS1*, but while the first game doesn't rule out the idea that the Age of Fire might continue indefinitely after the player's intervention, *DS2* undercuts all hopes of stability: regardless of the exact temporal relationship between the two games (which is a frequently debated point in the *DS* lore community), it is clear that the *DS* universe is stuck in a loop, with Ages of Fire and Dark in constant rotation. I will return to this cycle later in this chapter, but for now suffice it to say that by the time we reach the end of the game even the most attentive players are likely to have a vague idea at best of why they are there and how ending the curse would affect the game world and its larger lore. Put otherwise, the quest slides into the background of our experience as we approach its possible resolution. With remarkable self-awareness, *DS2* spells out this idea a number of times. A character known as the Firekeeper states at the start of the game: "One day you will stand before [the] decrepit gate [of Drangleic] without really knowing why." Much later, the Emerald Herald, who serves as our guide throughout the game, repeats the same idea: "Then, one day, you will walk those grounds without really knowing why." As the player progresses through the game, the purpose of their quest, already vague at the start, becomes more and more obscure: simultaneously, the path schema, which implies teleological movement and thus a clear set of goals, loses its grip on the player's experience. The loops that define both the Soulsring games' basic gameplay and their larger narrative universes contribute to this undermining of linearity, but so does the intricate system of side quests, as we will see in the next section.

Itinerant NPCs and Entangled Side Quests

In addition to the player-character's main story, the worlds of Soulsring games are rich in narratives centering on a large and varied cast of non-player characters (NPCs in short). Some of these are tragic figures who echo the apocalyptic framing of the Soulsring universe, while other NPCs introduce comic relief. In general, side quests reveal new aspects of the game's lore; some even lead to locations, boss fights, or weapons that we are not able to access otherwise. The distinction between the main storyline and the secondary missions or quests will be familiar to anyone who has experience with role-playing games (that is, the vast majority of *DS* or *ER* players). Typically, players advance a narrative by talking to certain characters, defeating an enemy, or solving spatial puzzles that unlock new areas of the game world. Some of these interactions develop the main quest and are thus needed to complete the game, whereas other interactions reveal stories that are self-contained and optional, even if they help flesh out the game's lore and atmosphere. What is unique about Soulsring games is that the distinction between main quest-advancing interactions and secondary stories is never made clear-cut or explicit. In most games, a quest menu will clearly set apart the main storyline from optional quests, with different categories for each and advanced tracking options (so that, for example, the player can filter out secondary quests on the map).

Soulsring games offer no such convenience. In *ER*, the player can go by the already mentioned "guidance of grace" icons on the map, which also shows the location of the NPCs involved in the side quests—but that is as user-friendly as the quest system gets. Previous *DS* games had no map and no way of tracking the NPCs' locations: it was entirely up to the player to remember where to find them, usually by drawing on community-created resources.[11] Moreover, NPCs in Soulsring games have a tendency to move around the world following the player's progress, which makes the task of keeping track of the storylines even more difficult.

Here is an example of the NPCs' volatility, from *ER*. Sometime after leaving the game's starting area, the player gains access to a location known as the Roundtable Hold, which serves a similar function to the Firelink Shrine in *DS* games: it is a hub allowing players to upgrade their weapons, purchase equipment, and encounter a number of key NPCs. One of these NPCs is a blindfolded character named Brother Corhyn, who is a follower of the religion known as the Golden Order and can teach spells based on the player-character's "faith" attribute ("incantations"). As the player progresses through the game world, Brother Corhyn decides to leave the Roundtable Hold. Instead, he can be found near a site of grace in Altus Plateau, where—he tells the player-character—he is looking for a mysterious scholar of the Golden Order, the "Noble Goldmask." As we explore the Altus Plateau, we come across Goldmask near a collapsed bridge north of Brother Corhyn's location (see figure 1.1). (Note that, given the size of the game world, it is perfectly possible to miss Goldmask unless we are actively pursuing this quest and using online guides to find them.) If we

Figure 1.1 Goldmask praying on a collapsed bridge in *Elden Ring*.

inform Brother Corhyn of Goldmask's location, he will move there, where we can talk to him for some additional lines of flavor text. The two will then reappear once the player has made it into Leyndell, the Royal Capital, where Goldmask is lost in contemplation of the Erdtree. Brother Corhyn asks for our help breaking the spell of Goldmask's silence. This involves solving a complicated puzzle somewhere else in Leyndell and then backtracking to Goldmask to reveal the secret we have just learned. Other than the Brother Corhyn icon on the map, the game gives us no means of keeping track of the quest and doesn't tell us how to advance it or where the two characters can be found next.

Moreover, while Brother Corhyn's quest is usually considered a "side" quest, completing it unlocks one of the game's endings: when we encounter Goldmask for the last time, we obtain the "Mending Rune of Perfect Order" that is needed for the Age of Order ending, in which, thanks to Goldmask's teachings, the player-character establishes an improved version of the Golden Order (which was shattered by events preceding the game's beginning).[12] In this way, the distinction between main and side stories is blurred not just in terms of how these quests are presented, but also at the level of the game's narrative workings: some of the best endings only become available by pursuing certain side quests in addition to what is generally regarded as the "main" story.

It is important to highlight that, as we play *ER*, we encounter a large number of NPCs like Brother Corhyn. Some lead to new endings, others are more self-contained, and there is essentially no way of knowing in advance who does what without consulting an internet guide. Further, it is extremely easy to accidentally spoil these quest lines either through missing an itinerant NPC's location or by selecting the wrong dialogue option. In some cases, the quest line will prematurely end and can only be completed by restarting the game. The NPCs thus create a network of quest lines that intersect and interact in unpredictable ways, sometimes converging with the main story, sometimes leading to narrative dead ends. In terms of Marie-Laure Ryan's (2006) types of narrative architecture (introduced at the beginning of the chapter), this structure closely resembles the maze, a highly nonlinear structure. The architecture of the side quests foregrounds image schemata of entanglement—both because the quests require constant backtracking and because the player is caught up or lost in a configuration that resists path-based understanding. Together with the lack of guidance on the level of the games' interface, the unpredictability of the quests contributes to disrupting the linearity of the narrative: not only can the side missions slow down the player's investment in the main story (which is a common experience in many games), but the sparse signposting and surprising outcomes of NPC stories make it difficult for players to know exactly on which path they are standing. More than the vast majority of role-playing games, *ER* immerses the player in an unpredictable, entangled narrative network.

Superimposition and Shadowtime: The Cosmological Frame

The narrative complexity of Soulsring games is further increased by the layering of backstories—where the idea of layering activates an image schema of superimposition, a stratification of temporalities that (in line with my account of complexity, see introduction) are simultaneously present in the player's experience. This superimposition starts with the ancient history of *DS* or *ER* myth, a "cosmological" frame that contextualizes the player-character's efforts. Soulsring games are rich in references to a mythical past, an "Age of the Ancients" in which the world was ruled by dragons. As the *DS* Wiki states: "In the Age of Ancients the world was unformed, shrouded by fog: a land of gray crags, Archtrees and Everlasting Dragons."[13] The lore surrounding these creatures is almost never directly discussed by the NPCs; instead, it is conveyed through physical traces in the games' environment and (even more sparsely) through item descriptions or cutscenes.[14] Perhaps more than anything else in the Soulsring universe, this cosmological framing calls for what I will call an "archaeological" mode of fandom, which denotes attention to environmental clues and an emotional investment in the material history of the game world.[15] Archaeological fandom and the literary nature of Soulsring games go hand in hand: the games' narrative rewards careful reconstruction and even speculation based on scant evidence, leading to a range of lore "theories" on the internet that blur the line between commentary, interpretation, and fan fiction.[16]

The layering of temporal planes in the Soulsring universe is frequently evoked by sections in which the player-character travels back in time. One of the most striking scenes from late-game *ER* takes the player back to the Age of the Ancients, if only for the duration of a boss encounter. The player is exploring a location known as Crumbling Farum Azula, a sprawling monumental complex overlooking a giant cyclone. Not only is Farum Azula physically separate from the Lands Between, but it appears to float in time as well: as a Reddit user puts it, the "events taking place there naturally are a mix of [echoes] of the past, and visions of the future."[17] An optional boss fight requires the player to climb down a series of ruins until they reach a broken stone platform where they see a "Lie down" prompt on the screen. As soon as they do so, a cutscene shows the ruins gradually returning to their original state, a large plaza surrounded by columns, with the Dragonlord Placidusax visible in the distance, expecting the player. Time changes direction here: the player travels back to the Age of the Ancients, where they face one of the Everlasting Dragons. This is one of the few direct references to the cosmological history of the *ER* world: the cutscene, with the plaza recomposing itself from broken stones, suggests that Soulsring landscapes always hover between the present and a distant past that can be reconstructed by archaeologically minded players. The broken platform in Farum Azula or the ruins that dot the world of Soulsring games serve as a physical reminder of a past that retains a ghostly presence, similar to the way in which other players' ghosts make brief appearances in our own world.[18]

Archaeologists Bjørnar Olsen, Michael Shanks, Timothy Webmoor, and Christopher Witmore (2012) use the metaphor of "percolation" to discuss how the layers that make up the archaeological record aren't sealed off but can (and typically do) influence one another. The idea of percolation captures how time seeps through the layers, with past events shaping the present and (in turn) present-day conceptions influencing our understanding of the past. The concept of percolation can be linked to the experience of "shadowtime," a term coined by Ranu Mukherjee and Alicia Escott (2015) as part of an art project known as the Bureau of Linguistical Reality. This artwork collects neologisms that describe unique feelings and thoughts arising in an era of climate uncertainty. Shadowtime, to quote from Mukherjee and Escott's definition, "manifests as a feeling of living in two distinctly different temporal scales simultaneously."[19] Environmental cues provided by Soulsring games are designed to create an experience of shadowtime as the player juggles multiple temporal planes, pointing simultaneously to the ancient history of the game world, its more recent past, the present moment, but also the future as determined by the player's decisions. With its confusion of temporalities and its references to the Age of the Ancients, Farum Azula serves as a striking example of temporal percolation: the Soulsring player is afforded an experience of shadowtime, of playing at a confluence of temporal planes.

In *DS2*, the "memories" encountered by the player also suggest superimposition of temporalities, even though they take the player back to a more recent past than the Age of the Ancients. But a link with the Ancients remains: the giants around which these flashbacks revolve are said to be related to the Ancient Dragons, perhaps as a reincarnation of their ancestral power.[20] Moreover, the item used to trigger the flashbacks, the Ashen Mist Heart, is obtained from a friendly Ancient Dragon; as typical in Soulsring games, the item description provides narrative context: "The magic of the ancient dragon allows one to delve into the memories of the withered." In this case, the "withered" are three giants fallen in battle during an invasion of Drangleic, earlier on in King Vendrick's reign and well before the events of the game. The memories are accessed, after collecting the Ashen Mist Heart, by interacting with the giants' seemingly fossilized corpses: as a result, the player travels back in time and witnesses key scenes in the giants' battle against King Vendrick. While these memories are named after three of the giants, they don't foreground individual experiences or perception so much as the spatial displacement of reliving some of the game's locations from a different historical perspective. This is another opportunity for an experience of shadowtime to arise: the memories evoke the historically stratified structure of Soulsring worlds, but also the possibility of resonances or echoes across the layers—especially if the player brings an archaeological mindset to the games. The cosmological frame and the recent past of the game world are thus interwoven into the player-character's present through highly suggestive flashbacks.

Just as the quest lines trace a network that challenges linear readings of the games, this tapestry of temporalities evokes an image schema of entanglement. Not only is time layered, but the layers are folded into one another, and sometimes that structure is made legible by the game world even outside of sequences that are explicitly marked as flashbacks. The regions of *ER*, for example, are punctuated by the collapsed remains of ancient structures that are visually reminiscent of Farum Azula: perhaps then the Farum Azula we visit in the course of our playthrough exists in a different timeline from the Farum Azula we see strewn across the landscape; or perhaps Farum Azula is the last standing "sky temple" of the many built before modern times, whose ruins are still visible (see Varnson 2022). Again, the uncertainty of the collapsed sky temple speaks to an archaeological mindset, encouraging the community to come up with theories as to the nature of these ruins—even if the game does very little to confirm or disconfirm the players' speculations. The entanglement schema isn't just evoked through time shifts, then, but also through physical structures that serve as a spatial stand-in for the layering of temporalities in the games (see chapter 2).

But we shouldn't forget that, particularly in *DS* games, history isn't merely a matter of superimposed temporal planes, since it is traversed by a cyclical dynamic: as I mentioned above, at the beginning of *DS1* the player is told that the Age of Fire will come to a close if the player-character doesn't act to save or "link" the First Flame. Regardless of whether the player decides to do so in the game's ending, *DS2* presents the player with an eerily similar choice, but in a different world: the same decision—whether to extend the Age of Fire or welcome a new Age of Dark—awaits the player at the end of the game, and *DS3* doesn't depart significantly from this template (see chapter 6). The conclusion proposed by many members of the *DS* community is that the games' universe traces a cycle, oscillating perpetually between light and darkness. This is how VaatiVidya puts it: referring to Gwyn, the god who ended the Age of the Ancients, he argues that he "forced the darkness back and from this moment forth, the light and the dark have been in a constant ebb and flow, like the rising and the falling of the tide."[21] Thus, alongside entanglement, cycle is another image schema that structures the player's understanding of *DS* temporality. In *ER*, cyclicity isn't suggested as strongly on a cosmological level, but that is an element that future expansions of the game world may still introduce.

***

We have seen in this chapter that Soulsring games implement multiple strategies to cue but also destabilize an understanding of narrative temporality modeled on the path image schema: from the underlying difficulty of the games, which forces players to tackle the same areas in repetitive loops, to the crisscrossing structure of secondary quest lines, the games trace a uniquely complex narrative structure. Work in film studies shows such nonlinearity at work in contemporary cinema and TV, identifying a number of alternative image schemata (from containment to entanglement) that help audiences navigate this complexity. But there are also striking differences in the degree to which these nonlinear image schemata leave the audience with a sense of closure. In puzzle-like complexity, all the pieces fit together neatly: provided that the viewer is willing to invest the cognitive effort, a nonlinear narrative can be rearranged within a sufficiently coherent structure. By contrast, in more open-ended uses of complexity, the disruption of the path model remains suspended and susceptible to various (and possibly conflicting) interpretations. This type of complexity favors "real mysteries" over puzzles, to adopt Abbott's (2013) terminology. Here, nonlinear image schemata may offer glimpses of narrative coherence: the loop of Soulsring death cycles, for example, or the rotation of Age of Fire and Age of Dark in *DS* cosmology present circular schemata as a possible alternative to linearity. However, it is impossible for players to fully reconcile these loops with the entanglement schema of the side quests or the overlapping temporal planes of the narrative's past, present, and future. The three schemata (loop, entanglement, superimposition) remain active in the player's experience, disrupting the path-like linearity of the player-character's main quest and creating a sense of complex stratification or layering, which I have described in this chapter through metaphors such as percolation and shadowtime. In Soulsring games, time is convoluted because numerous temporal planes are interwoven in an unpredictable, uncertain manner, with the cosmological past emerging periodically from both the physical landscape of the game world and strategic flashbacks—but never coalescing into an explicit backstory that the player could take at face value. This mythical frame interacts with the more recent history of the game worlds as well as with the player's own attempts to determine the fate of this universe through their decision making.

This layered temporal structure calls for an archaeological mode of fandom; it also factors into the literary complexity of these games as I have defined it in the introduction. The narrative complexity of Soulsring games cultivates attention to seemingly minor aspects of the game worlds, such as item descriptions and physical environments, which serve as the basis for creative reconstruction and narrative-based speculation. There is no simple way of "cracking" this mystery; instead, negotiating the temporality of *DS* games and *ER* involves developing an appreciation of its open-endedness and also welcoming the diversity of interpretations offered by the community. In order to understand the community-driven nature of Soulsring meaning making, though, it is important to complement this discussion of temporality with insight into the equally complex way in which these games make use of physical space. I turn to this spatial layer of complexity in the next chapter.

Notes

1 https://www.reddit.com/r/darksouls3/comments/5padvi/lore_flow_of_time_which_world_are_we_in/. The post takes a humorous twist halfway through, but the continuity problem identified by dylanalduin is (as many responses to their post attest) a serious one, and shared by many players.

2 I offer a more sustained account of how the teleology of the protagonist's goals steers narrative in Caracciolo (2021, chap. 2), building on Marie-Laure Ryan's (1991) approach to plot.

3 See Schniedermann (2023) for a discussion of the time loop form in a number of contemporary works, including *Russian Doll*.

4 On image schemata, see the collection edited by Hampe and Grady (2005). On image schemata for time specifically, see Boroditsky (2000).

5 See this post from 2018 for the online death count: https://www.reddit.com/r/DarkSouls2/comments/a5iu6b/the_death_counter_in_majula_recently_hit_300/.

6 See Jayemanne (2017, 271): "Some games, such as *Dark Souls* … , make progress much more precarious … and thereby give more emphasis to particular performances. The save function is not simply an auxiliary compensation for real-world limitations on play time, but a synchronizing process that, in its specificity, can have a powerful effect on a given performance and the experience of play."

7 See Lahdenperä (2018) and Caracciolo (2022c) for further discussion of the link between time loop narrative and video games. Hanson's (2018, chap. 6) account of recursive temporality in games is also relevant here.

8 The player-character, also known as "avatar," is a representation that players control directly and that allows them to interact with the game world—for example, by collecting resources or fighting other players or computer-controlled enemies (see Vella 2013).

9 https://youtu.be/2hwCGxhFOlM.

10 See, e.g., https://www.reddit.com/r/DarkSouls2/comments/2fghhs/undead_curse_i_want_to_understand_you_but/.

11 For more on the integration of in-game experience and community resources, see chapter 4.

12 I will discuss the game's endings in more detail in chapter 6.

13 https://darksouls.fandom.com/wiki/Age_of_Ancients.

14 I will return to the environmental storytelling of Soulsring games in chapter 2.

15 I introduced this terminology in Caracciolo (2022b). See also Bennett et al. (2023) for a convergent discussion of archaeology and video games.

16 For two stimulating examples of cosmological speculation, see the following posts: https://www.reddit.com/r/darksouls/comments/erv0zo/dark_souls_origins_explaining_the_age_of_ancients/ and https://www.reddit.com/r/darksouls3/comments/4i19oh/lore_overall_dark_souls_theory_giant/.

17 https://www.reddit.com/r/Eldenring/comments/vb4d53/lore_behind_farum_azula/.

18 I will have more to say about these ghosts in chapter 4.

19 For an application of the shadowtime concept to literary reading, see Lambert (2022).

20 See https://www.reddit.com/r/DarkSouls2/comments/26imf6/i_get_it_nowtheory_on_dragons_and_ancient_giants/.

21 https://youtu.be/Cdk_fvXG5xA.

2 Game Space

Layers and Gaps

"Games celebrate and explore spatial representation as their central motif and *raison d'être*," writes Espen Aarseth (2007, 161), an idea that is echoed by many scholars who have developed sophisticated conceptual tools for the study of video game spaces. The main function of these tools is to identify differences or levels within the player's engagement with digital spatiality, which (especially when immersed in a game) can feel perfectly continuous and seamless. On a closer look, though, the space of video games isn't a continuum but presents a highly segmented and layered structure. Soulsring games make effective use of this stratification, particularly through interactions between storytelling, gameplay, and the experiential qualities of the spaces they foreground. These interactions, as I will argue in this chapter, greatly contribute to the games' literary complexity.

To understand the specificities of the Soulsring treatment of game space (as well as differences across Soulsring games), we need to take a step back and survey work on the general features of video game spatiality. An article by Huaxin Wei, Jim Bizzocchi, and Tom Calvert (2010) provides a helpful synthesis of narratological and game design-oriented scholarship on space. Adapting Gabriel Zoran's (1984) work on narrative space in fiction, Wei, Bizzocchi, and Calvert distinguish between three levels of spatial structure in games. The first level is the *topographic* one: this is a top-down representation of game space as "static and independent of both plot enactment and screen representation" (2010, 8). Topographic space can be seen as the sum total of the spaces portrayed by a game; clearly, this isn't a space that players will experience as such, but rather an idealization or conceptual model that they will use to navigate game spaces. Wei, Bizzocchi, and Calvert identify two factors in the topographic (that is, global) organization of game spaces: layout and oppositions. The layout has to do with the overall structure of space, for example, whether it is constructed according to a linear logic (as in a side-scrolling platformer, where the end of the level is typically to the right of the starting point), it is maze-like (as in many first-person shooters), or it has a more open configuration (as in many role-playing games).[1] Spatial oppositions are frequently used in game design to diversify the topology of the game world, for example, by

DOI: 10.4324/9781032684024-3

distinguishing the areas where combat takes place from safe areas in which players interact with friendly NPCs (e.g., in *DS* games, Firelink Shrine).

The second level discussed by Wei, Bizzocchi, and Calvert is the *operational* one, which refers to game spaces as apprehended by the player through navigation and exploration. This dimension is closer to space as actually experienced on a moment-by-moment basis. The player's traversal of game space can follow one or more routes, depending on the topological layout of the game world: in an open-world game like *The Witcher 3: Wild Hunt* (CD Projekt RED 2015), players can (and frequently do) retrace their footsteps, for instance, in order to advance quests or collect their rewards. In other games, however, paths can be traversed in one direction only: there is no going back or revisiting previous locations. But the player is not the only entity to move within game spaces: as Wei, Bizzocchi, and Calvert note, objects and NPCs can move, too, and their mobility (or lack thereof) often determines the direction of the player's own explorations. (As we will see, the spatial complexity of Soulsring games has to do, among other factors, with how unpredictable the NPCs' movements can be.) Finally, the third level is the *presentational* one, which concerns the techniques that enable the audiovisual representation of the game world. The interface plays a major role on this level: some games feature a map or a mini-map superimposed on the game world, or alternatively a compass with quest markers. These navigational tools are typically accompanied by an audiovisual viewpoint, which can be fixed or player-controlled (as in a cinematic camera) and introduces a distinction between on-screen and off-screen space.

Topographic, operational, and presentational dimensions jointly shape players' experience of spatiality in games. Although Wei, Bizzocchi, and Calvert don't discuss this point, players are likely to start from a certain set of assumptions surrounding topography, which can be based on game-specific expectations created by the community or can reflect their familiarity with the game's genre. This topographic model is then updated (and if necessary revised) according to the way in which spaces are presented and made operational while navigating the game world. If the topographic layout is a top-down, global model imposed on game worlds, the player's experience of operational space (as well as its presentation at the level of game interface) can influence this schema and even invite players to adjust their initial topographic model.[2] In that respect, game spatiality isn't fundamentally different from our experience of real space, which is riddled with gaps that point to both discontinuities in scale and varying emotional and cultural investments in space. In games, spatial discontinuities often emerge as players attempt to triangulate their topographic model with the operational and presentational dimensions of space: for instance, an in-game map may include areas that are not (yet) accessible to players, or the general topography of the game world may suggest freedom of movement despite posing significant operational constraints on the player.

Here is an example of discontinuity from the level design of FromSoftware games: Soulsring games frequently tease the player with valuable items that appear to be close and within reach but cannot actually be accessed from the player's current location. Getting to these items tends to involve roundabout routes or hidden passages; in short, the game world is laid out in such a way that proximity doesn't always imply accessibility, because to collect these items the player has to move *away* from them (and of course, there is always the possibility of the player forgetting about the item or missing it entirely). This strategy builds on a gap between the topography of the game world (which affords the player a certain freedom of movement) and the operational dimension of the player's traversal, which cannot be simply mapped onto the visual topography but follows a different, more indirect logic.

Such spatial discrepancies are common in games; players have learned to expect them as part of the "gappiness" of any simulative system. In Ian Bogost's words, "There is a space or a gap between which the key to approaching and understanding simulations might be found. This gap constitutes the core representation of simulation, between the work's rules and its reception" (2006, 107). Nevertheless, not all gaps are equally meaningful in the experience of game spaces. I will argue in this chapter that Soulsring games use discontinuities between topographic, operational, and presentational dimensions of space in uniquely challenging ways, and that such spatial challenges form an essential part of these games' appeal and sophistication. These discontinuities exist on a number of levels: they affect the possibly unreliable item descriptions that play a central role in the games' storytelling; they emerge within the games' affectively complex atmosphere, which brings together diverse emotional registers such as the sublime and the apocalyptic; and gaps are also created by the NPCs' tendency to move around in space in an unpredictable manner. Before elaborating on that reading, we need to consider how narrative enters spatial relations in Soulsring games. That requires introducing discussions on video games and narrative and then homing in on the spatial nature of game storytelling. To illuminate some of those issues, I will turn to and refine Henry Jenkins's concept of environmental storytelling and adapt it to FromSoftware games.

Narrative in Game Spaces

Discussions on the narrativity of video games can be traced back to the early days of game studies, when game researchers were attempting to define the boundaries of the field and also claim the unique features of the game medium vis-à-vis pre-digital media (such as literature and film). Game narrative was caught in the crossfire of what went down in game studies history as a debate between "ludologists" and "narratologists," but it was actually the former—particularly scholars such as Markku Eskelinen (2001) and Gonzalo Frasca (2003a)—who shaped the discussion. Narratologists were a more loosely defined group that included Janet Murray (1998) and Marie Laure-Ryan (2001)—scholars whose work approached games by building on (but also adapting and extending) existing conceptual tools, such as those of narratology. The debate has been revisited a number of times (see Frasca 2003b), so it seems unnecessary to reconstruct it in detail here. Suffice it to say that, in hindsight, the ludologists' main goal was to avoid the uncritical extension of literary studies-based concepts to the digital medium: instead, they highlighted the ludic nature of video games and their continuity with other forms of rule-based play (for instance, boardgames). Today, the debate has largely subsided and scholars in both narrative theory (M.-L. Ryan 2006; Punday 2019) and game studies have started theorizing about the role of narrative in gameplay in less dichotomous ways. Ryan puts it succinctly: "computer games are an art of compromise between narrative and gameplay" (2006, 198). This compromise can take numerous forms, and there are undoubtedly many instances of gameplay in which narrative isn't central to game mechanics or to the player's experience. But there are also games—narrative-focused games, I call them in Caracciolo (2015, 234)—that foreground storytelling to the degree that the experience of the game appears far less rewarding if the player ignores the narrative dimension.

Soulsring games occupy a unique position on this spectrum. Their ludic mechanics—particularly the combat, but also the exploration and spatial puzzle-solving—create challenges and offer rewards independently of any emotional investment in the layers of narrativity I have examined in the previous chapter. It is, in other words, perfectly possible to spend countless hours playing Soulsring games without devoting any attention to the narratives they weave. But to players who are willing to spend the time and effort to tease out the games' narrativity, there are significant emotional benefits to be reaped. Again, the archaeological metaphor can be useful here: because so much narrative content is obscure or carefully hidden away (for instance, in item descriptions), the player is encouraged to piece together scant clues and come up with theories that only (and at best) receive partial confirmation in the course of a playthrough. One may be tempted to compare this approach to what Jason Mittell calls "forensic fandom" in a discussion of complex TV: "Complex television encourages forensic fans to dig deeper, probing beneath the surface to understand the complexity of a story and its telling" (2015, 288). The word "forensic" brings up the possibility of closure, it hints at a mystery that can be solved—not a "real mystery" (in Abbott's sense) that remains recalcitrant to reconstruction or interpretation. This is why I prefer the archaeological metaphor to the forensic one; for Olsen, Shanks, Webmoor, and Witmore, archaeological work revolves around care defined as the "painstaking toll of cleaning, examining, and conserving artifacts by technicians and curators" (2012, 66). This type of care isn't necessarily aimed at producing answers or solutions in the sense of a forensic investigation: although archaeologists do come up with explanations and hypotheses, their work is centered on the preservation of a past whose interpretation remains, as Olsen, Shanks, Webmoor, and Witmore highlight, fundamentally unstable and open-ended.[3]

Similarly, narratively minded players of Soulsring games are constantly on the lookout for clues that can help them reconstruct a layered past. But the complexity of these entangled narratives cannot be simply "solved," as we have seen in the previous chapter. Instead, the player is encouraged to adopt an archaeologist's mindset, collecting clues and working out fragments of story that never crystallize into a coherent or overarching narrative. There can still be consensus about *some* aspects of the games' narratives, of course: the NPCs' quest lines, for example, typically come close to a well-formed narrative with a beginning, a middle, and an end, although a few questions are likely to linger. By contrast, what I called the games' "cosmological" plot remains shrouded in uncertainty, fueling internet speculation but resisting any definitive answer. Thus, the type of archaeological fandom that focuses on the games' narratives tends to blur the boundary between lore "theories" and full-blown fan fiction. Many players find these creative engagements deriving from the games' uncertain narrative at least as rewarding as the ludic interactions of Soulsring combat.

In his early article on *DS1*, Vella introduced the phrase "ludic sublime" to capture the peculiar form of mystery that defines the *DS* experience (for him, and arguably for all narrative-minded players). *DS*, Vella contends, "works to actively remind the player of the limits and the inadequacy of her perceptual opening onto the milieu of the gameworld, the computational systems underlying it, and the space of possibilities they structure" (2015). The sublime is here conceptualized as imperviousness to comprehension, a response that (following again Vella's argumentation) *DS1* elicits through three formal techniques: a lack of segmentation of game space, so that (for example) the boundary between starting and high-level areas remains largely unmarked; the ambiguity of the game's systems, particularly in terms of unclear or disrupted linkages between the players' actions and their effects; and what Vella calls "ergodic irony," which has to do with how the game constantly reminds us of the opportunities we missed or the actions we decided not to take.

Vella's approach offers a number of useful insights into the game's affect, but it tends to downplay the specific contribution of storytelling to the ludic sublime. In *DS1* and in all other Soulsring games, adopting an archaeological mode of gameplay reveals the depth and intricacy of the narratives. However, because of the recalcitrant nature of the games' storytelling, the narrative-minded player cannot achieve closure but has to hold on to a humbling feeling of partial comprehension. This sublime effect is closely bound up with the spatiality of the game worlds, and particularly with how spaces consistently cue narrative meaning making without providing clear-cut answers.

Henry Jenkins's (2004) influential discussion of environmental storytelling in games can be helpful here. While repeatedly framed as a "narratologist" in the early game studies debate, Jenkins's concept actually identifies a means of delivering narrative that is unique to games. For Jenkins, space is *the* essential dimension of games: thoughtful game design is fundamentally about constructing spaces for satisfying (if challenging) interactions. The best way to tell stories within these environments isn't in the form of verbal or audiovisual exposition, which disrupts the flow of the player's interactions. Rather, Jenkins focuses on the benefits of what he calls "spatial stories," which "can evoke pre-existing narrative associations; they can provide a staging ground where narrative events are enacted; they may embed narrative information within their mise-en-scene; or they provide resources for emergent narratives" (2004, 123). What exactly is a spatial story, however? Jenkins's concept refers broadly to the way in which storytelling can enter digital spaces, for instance by evoking stories players are already familiar with through earlier narrative interactions (as in one of Jenkins's examples, American McGee's 2000 video game adaptation of Lewis Carroll's *Alice in Wonderland*). But the main takeaway of Jenkins's discussion is that, in games, "essential narrative information must be presented redundantly across a range of spaces and artifacts, because one cannot assume the player will necessarily locate or recognize the significance of any given element" (2004, 126). The setting thus becomes directly expressive or evocative of narrative through spatial scenes or objects that encourage narrativization on the part of the player.[4]

Compare this approach to a cinematic narrative technique adopted by many games, the use of prerendered sequences known as "cutscenes." These scenes suspend interactivity to display a fixed event sequence, either at the beginning of the game (to set up the plot) or at key junctures. Cutscenes of this kind take the agency away from players, uncoupling ludic action from *narrative* action—and thus cementing a divide between narrativity and gameplay. Instead, environmental storytelling works toward reducing this divide, since spatial stories don't suspend interactivity but rather present players with a choice: paying attention to the narrative content that is bound up with certain spatial features or continuing to foreground the ludic dimension of gameplay. Whatever the player decides, the fact that an experience of player agency is maintained deepens the integration between the game's environment and its storytelling potential: this integration represents the main advantage of environmental storytelling in games.

Typically, spatial stories come in two flavors. Some involve verbal or audiovisual media that are distributed across the game world in the form of audio or video recordings or written notes. By reading or otherwise interacting with these documents, the player gains insight into the history of the game world and its characters' backstories. Numerous examples of this media-based environmental storytelling can be found in the indie game *Gone Home* (The Fullbright Company 2013). The game starts with the player character arriving at her family home in Oregon after a long absence, only to discover that the house is deserted. On the main door she finds a note from her sister begging the protagonist not to investigate the events that led to the family's abrupt departure. Naturally, the player-character decides to do the opposite, exploring the house's vast interior and uncovering a wide range of media objects (from an answering machine to letters and magazines) that gradually reveal the game's plot. This is environmental storytelling in its purest form, since direct interaction with in-game artifacts is the main (or only) factor guiding the player's narrative meaning making. In that sense, the environmental storytelling of *Gone Home* illustrates Marie-Laure Ryan's concept of "exploratory interactivity" (2006, 113), in which the player uses a variety of clues to reconstruct a story that predates their engagement with the game world.

A second type of environmental storytelling is more diffuse and depends less on semiotic artifacts than on nonverbal environmental traces. Clara Fernández-Vara's (2011) phrase "interpretation of remains" refers to environmental storytelling in general but might actually be better suited to describe this second type, in which spatial stories are not tied to semiotic media but rather to physical traces that function indexically—that is, by materially pointing to an event that took place in the same environment.[5] In this indexical storytelling, the integration of spatial setting and narrative is even tighter than in the previous type, because it is not mediated by full-fledged semiotic artifacts but rather tied to material clues or marks. For example, in Lucas Pope's game *Return of the Obra Dinn* (Pope 2018), the player is tasked with investigating what happened on the titular ship, which was recovered with all crew members dead or missing. The player-character boards the ship, examines the crew members' remains, and can use a special watch to rewind time and travel back to their moment of death. These flashbacks present the player with relatively static snapshots of temporal experience, usually in highly emotionally charged situations (a violent altercation between two crew members, a kraken attacking the ship). Through their emotional value, these sequences trigger the "human tendency to insert narrative time into static, immobile scenes" (Abbott 2008, 7).[6] In *Return of the Obra Dinn*, this "insertion" requires paying close attention to mostly nonverbal elements of the represented situation, such as the relative positioning of the characters on the ship, what weapons can be found in the vicinity of the characters' bodies, and so on.

To recap, environmental storytelling in games builds on a close integration of spatial and narrative cues, so that the plot doesn't appear to originate externally to the players' interactions but rather arises from within our navigation of the game world—what Wei, Bizzocchi, and Calvert refer to as the "operational space." Concretely, spatially distributed stories in games can take two different forms: they can be conveyed by verbal or audiovisual artifacts, or they can be tied to physical elements or traces that suggest what happened in the same space at an earlier time. These categories are certainly not mutually exclusive, since many games resort to both techniques to evoke narratively layered situations. Soulsring games are among them. As we will see, the gappiness of their environmental storytelling amplifies the complexity of their game worlds and sets the player's interpretive meaning making in motion.

Item Descriptions and Unreliable Narrative

While Soulsring games feature occasional cutscenes, this cinematic device is used much more sparingly than in other role-playing games. Typically, the games start with a cutscene in which a voiceover narrator briefly outlines the history of the world the player is thrown into—what I called its "cosmology" in the previous chapter—and names the main enemies we will face in the course of the playthrough.[7] More cutscenes introduce the key boss fights, but there is usually no voiceover here: the primary function of these sequences isn't storytelling but rather characterization (presenting the enemy the player is up against), along with raising expectations for a difficult fight. Finally, the games close with a cutscene corresponding to the players' chosen ending: these are mainly visual sequences that, like so much about Soulsring games, provide closure and ambiguity in equal parts, particularly ambiguity about the exact ramifications of the ending the player has triggered.

Some more narrative cues are provided by dialogue with the NPCs as the player follows the games' intersecting quest lines, but the vast majority of the narrative content of Soulsring games is delivered via the items the player comes across in the game world. These items include the weapons or armor obtained by killing certain enemies or other quest-advancing items such as physical keys, medallions, and so on. Collecting and curating these objects speaks to the archaeological mode of engagement I have already introduced. Not all of these items are equally valuable from a narrative perspective, though: in general, the more challenging and salient the boss encounter, the more narratively significant the descriptions of the items obtained after the fight. For example, most *DS2* bosses drop special "souls," which can be exchanged for either a large number of regular souls (the in-game currency allowing players to level up) or powerful weapons. When the player kills an early game boss, the "Dragonrider," they can collect an item called the "Dragonrider Soul." Accessed through the inventory interface, the description of this item reads as follows: "Soul of a Dragonrider, who faithfully served King Vendrick. Long ago, the dragonriders mounted wyrms, and were feared on the battlefield for their unparalleled strength."[8] This is an important piece of information linking the Dragonrider to King Vendrick, one of the story's main characters, who will make a striking appearance later on in the playthrough. The description also introduces the historical depth of the game world ("long ago"), thus evoking the temporal layering discussed in the previous chapter. This is a strategy implemented pervasively by Soulsring games, which contain hundreds of items, each with its own textual description accessible through the game's interface.

The player is, of course, free to ignore the descriptions or approach them with an archaeological mindset, reading them closely and using them to piece together the characters' relationships and backstories—a widespread practice in Soulsring communities on Reddit or YouTube. The descriptions constitute environmental storytelling in that these items are scattered throughout the game world or dropped by the bosses we kill along the way, as a "remembrance" of the battle (*ER* uses precisely this word for the item type equivalent to *DS* "boss souls").

This embedding of textual material within the operational space of the game is reminiscent of what I called the media-based type of environmental storytelling, but it also departs from this model in two ways. First, because the text can be displayed only by opening the in-game inventory, the divide between gameplay and narrative is to some extent preserved: rather than engaging with a semiotic artifact directly (as in the case of *Gone Home*, where the player can physically pick up and manipulate letters or other documents within the game world), the player has to interact with an in-game menu to access the item descriptions, which is a far more indirect way of taking in an environmental story. The spatial embedding of these stories is still present, largely through the location or situation in which the items have been recovered by the player; but the narrative clues provided by the descriptions exist in an interface (presentational) space distinct from the operational space of gameplay.

Even more unusually, though, the vast majority of items responsible for environmental storytelling in Soulsring games are *not* semiotic artifacts, because it is never suggested that the text of the descriptions is physically or digitally inscribed on the items themselves. Rather, the text appears to originate externally, perhaps from the voice of a heterodiegetic Soulsring narrator who provides interested players with tidbits of narrative. It is certainly possible to identify this narrator with the voiceover of the opening cutscenes: while the identification is never supported by the game, at first glance the descriptions do seem to display the authorial gravitas we associate with the narrator of the opening.[9] Indeed, as already mentioned, the descriptions are in many instances the only source players can use to reconstruct the games' narrative lore. The problem, however, is that on closer analysis the descriptions prove to be anything but a reliable, authorial source. Reddit user TKeep, for instance, notes that there are "moments when physical remains [i.e., what I am calling the item descriptions] contradict the 'official' narrative presented through dialogue or cut scene narration."[10]

As an example of these discrepancies, another user (GhoulInDisguise) mentions the case of a recurring *DS* character named Havel. A *DS1* item, the Watchtower Basement Key, states that "the basement of the watchtower forms a stone cell. There are rumors of a hero turned Hollow who was locked away by a dear friend."[11] When the player enters the stone cell and kills the character there, they collect an item named "Havel's ring," and they may infer from this label that the "hero" they have just defeated was Havel himself. However, the ring description actually refers to "Havel's men [who] wore the ring to express faith in their leader."[12] In other words, the enemy we fought may not be the "hero" we were promised by the Watchtower Basement Key description, but a mere follower. In a different Reddit thread, user SundownKid notes, in response to a similar query about the possibly unreliable item descriptions, that the flavor text is "definitely not the absolute truth. There are numerous examples of the descriptions being incorrect."[13] If the descriptions originate from a heterodiegetic narrator, this must be an unreliable narrator who deliberately misreports or obfuscates some facts in order to mislead the player.[14] This realization complicates the already challenging task of reconstructing the games' narrative, because our main source of environmental storytelling (and of storytelling more generally) in the games turns out to be partial and perhaps even flawed.

Players can, of course, respond in multiple ways to the narrator's unreliability. First, the unreliability may go completely unnoticed: after all, only players willing to sift through multiple item descriptions—that is, players whose interest in the games is primarily geared toward archaeological fandom—will stumble upon these inconsistencies. If these inconsistencies are noticed, however, one option is to appeal to what Tamar Yacobi (1981) calls the "genetic principle" for dealing with textual oddities. This principle, as Yacobi states, "resolves fictive oddities and inconsistencies in terms of the causal factors that produced the text without coming to form part of it: the creative process, the history of the finished product, and above all the situation and tendencies of the historical producer" (1981, 114). The genetic strategy is easily applied to a product as complex as a video game, in which the writing originates from multiple individuals working collaboratively—a collective form of authorship where minor inconsistencies (particularly given the vastness of the games' macrotext) are highly likely to fall through the cracks of quality control. Adopting a similar genetic approach, a Reddit user (PKM1111) points to mistranslation from the games' Japanese original as a source of these incongruities.[15]

Other ways of dealing with the item descriptions take the inconsistencies at face value instead of dismissing them as a byproduct of game creation. For instance, in the same subreddit as PKM1111, user ChinaChina14 argues that "the descriptions reflect the ideas and beliefs of the people at the time," suggesting that these descriptions do not derive from a single narrative voice but rather from a collective whose understanding of the game world's history has evolved over time. The focus on collectivity is thus transposed from the collaborative nature of the writing process to the fictional level of the item descriptions' narrator. This, again, evokes the stratified complexity of Soulsring games' lore, how it resists capture within a linear schema.

Alternatively, players may adopt what Yacobi (1981, 117) calls the "functional principle," which involves reading unreliable elements as fulfilling a thematic function. In this case, the clashing item descriptions would play into Vella's ludic sublime: they would amplify the player's lack of comprehension and thus the emotional effects of games that embrace difficulty not only in gameplay terms (as widely recognized), but also in narrative terms.[16]

I mentioned above that the environmental storytelling of Soulsring games creates an unusual distance between operational space (the game world as explored by the player) and the games' interface, in which the item descriptions are contained. Further, the narratorial source of these descriptions generates uncertainty, which is of course only deepened by the unreliability players may notice if they start scrutinizing these texts. The unreliability is striking because it undermines ideas of authenticity associated with environmental storytelling: in the world of *Gone Home*, for example, discovering a handwritten note lends poignancy to the protagonist's emotional distress as she realizes that her family disappeared in mysterious circumstances. This is due to the simulated materiality of the letter, which brings together the physical space of the game and two emotionally connoted timelines: the present in which the note is found and the past of the note's composition. In Soulsring games, by contrast, the environmental storytelling creates more gaps than it closes; these discontinuities are simultaneously spatial and narrative, since they highlight both the distinction between operational and presentational space (the environment and the interface) and the impossibility of fully reconstructing the games' story. When these incongruities are experienced by the players, they open up a space for reflecting on and interpreting the sophisticated and highly ambiguous narrative design.

Atmosphere and Moving Bodies

Item descriptions are the most straightforward source of environmental storytelling in Soulsring games, but the physical layout of the game worlds—their topography, in Wei, Bizzocchi, and Calvert's sense—can tell spatial stories, too. This narrative potential of location is a function of multiple design choices, starting from what we may refer to as the atmosphere of Soulsring games. I am inspired here by Hans Ulrich Gumbrecht's account of "reading for *Stimmung*," which entails "paying attention to the textual dimension of the forms that envelop us and our bodies as a physical reality—something that can catalyze inner feelings without matters of representation necessarily being involved" (2012, 5). There can be little doubt that Soulsring games are highly atmospheric. On a subreddit, user ZenXw describes this atmosphere as a "mixture of loneliness, awe inspiring, sublime, sadness and hope."[17] While Soulsring games offer numerous images of devastation—among them abandoned towns, deserted castles, and inhospitable swamps—there is far more than bleakness at play. ZenXw captures the affective complexity of the games, how they can inspire a sense of sublime (a version of Vella's ludic sublime) and even hope *despite* the darkness that surrounds the player. In the same Reddit thread, Kapitaen_Sturzflug agrees with ZenXw and adds that the game's "difficulty is also a great part of it"—suggesting perhaps that the rewards of the challenging gameplay make up for the unwelcoming nature of the landscape. Another Reddit user, Temias, links the uniqueness of *DS1*'s atmosphere to the sparseness of the narrative: "The experience isn't aggressive or limited in how well it's told, because it's not told in a conventional way at all… . There's a weird sense of immersion, and with it comes a certain amount of sadness, loneliness, and stress." Still, it is clear from the discussion that—for these players at least—the bleakness led to a sense of enjoyment and even "weird immersion," an image that resonates with Gumbrecht's remarks on the enveloping quality of atmosphere.

Atmosphere is of course not the same as environmental storytelling, but there is a great deal of narrative potential in the mixed affect evoked by Soulsring games, the blend of despair and sublimity discussed by ZenXw. This affective tension leads to an experiential (atmospheric) instability that makes space for storytelling. Paraphrasing Tzvetan Todorov's (1968) structuralist work, David Herman argues that narratives "characteristically follow a trajectory leading from an initial state of equilibrium, through a phase of disequilibrium, to an endpoint at which equilibrium is restored (on a different footing) because of intermediary events" (2009, 96). The affectively complex atmosphere of Soulsring games cannot restore equilibrium by itself, but it can approximate the first two steps of Todorov's sequence by alternating hope and despair, sublimity and bleakness. Consider, for example, an area in *ER* known as "Liurnia of the Lakes." Our first impression of this area, after defeating the boss in Stormveil Castle, is steeped in the sublime: from a bluff, we take in a vast expanse of lakes and forests shrouded in fog, a castle visible in the distance (see figure 2.1). But despite this fairy tale-like appearance, entering Liurnia reveals a far bleaker picture: the landscape is punctuated by ruins, and a whole town (the Temple Quarter) appears to be sinking into the marshy terrain, with only a few roofs or taller buildings emerging from the ground. Through its visual and affective contrasts, this type of landscape inspires the attitude that Fernández-Vara (2011) labels "interpretation of remains," which is closely correlated with what I have described as archaeological fandom in Soulsring games. The landscape takes on narrative potential through the uneasy atmosphere it creates: the player first observes a grand vista (creating an affective equilibrium), but closer exploration reveals a wasteland that challenges that first impression (hence the disequilibrium). The player wonders why these ruins are here, why the buildings are sinking, what role the neighboring castle might have played in the devastation. In the tension between those affective stances, an opportunity arises for environmental storytelling of the indexical type, which focuses on physical traces

Figure 2.1 A view of Liurnia of the Lakes in *Elden Ring*.

and remains. The topography of the game world thus accommodates a series of affective contrasts that generate spatial stories in an inchoate form.

The quest lines of Soulsring games, which are also spatially distributed, typically tap into this atmospheric potential and articulate it through more explicit narrative. Just south of *ER*'s starting location, the player finds an area called the "Weeping Peninsula." An anonymous user on the Fextralife website describes the atmospheric qualities of this place as follows: "You are standing in a dull, gray, crumbling graveyard on a tiny island crowned by a long-dead tree. You are surrounded by nothing but water and half-submerged ruins… . I've definitely stood in that small graveyard for a while, just taking in the atmosphere of that area."[18] The toponym "Weeping" ostensibly refers to the atmospheric fact that it is always raining on the Peninsula, but a quest line taking place around Castle Morne on the Peninsula amplifies and specifies the gloominess of this place. The player first runs into a character named Irina, who asks them to deliver a letter to her father, Edgar, the embattled commander of Castle Morne (which is about to be taken over by hostile forces). When the player reaches the castle and hands over the letter, Irina's father remarks that he cannot join Irina until the leader of the invaders is defeated. After killing this enemy, players realize that Edgar has left the castle. Expecting a happy ending, they visit Irina's location again, only to discover Edgar prostrate by Irina's dead body: the implication is that he arrived too late to save her from the invaders. As in many other Soulsring quest lines, this tragic outcome is unavoidable and completely independent of player action, although players may miss Irina's death completely if they fail to travel back to her location. The quest line ends much later in the game, in Liurnia, where players face a hostile version of Edgar, who attacks them after losing his sanity. Irina's narrative thus foregrounds the player's tragic inability to alter the course of the events—a sense of ineluctability that builds on the dismal atmosphere of the Weeping Peninsula and fleshes it out through a relatively compact and overt (at least by Soulsring standards) narrative.

The name of the Peninsula thus hints at a deep connection between the atmospheric qualities of this landscape and the type of stories that can take place there. While in the case of Liurnia the environmental storytelling works by indexically referring to the past (when, for example, the Temple Quarter was not half-submerged), the name "Weeping Peninsula" projects that indexicality into the future by announcing the tragic affect of Irina's death *before* that event occurs in the game's timeline. Also significant here is how the game's environmental storytelling takes advantage of the NPCs' mobility: players travel back to Edgar's previous location but find that he has moved somewhere else. In this instance, it is not hard to guess where Edgar might be (by Irina's body), but in the case of longer and more complicated quest lines it can prove quite a challenge for the player, because NPCs have a tendency to travel much farther afield. If we don't want to miss an important step, we are forced to either use online resources or scour the game's vast world for clues. The game's topographic space becomes a stage for an unpredictable kind of environmental storytelling, in which the NPCs' moving bodies point, indexically, to our progression within a given quest line. In many instances, this forces the player to backtrack in order to advance a quest—a strategy that, as seen in the previous chapter, complicates the linearity built into the concept of quest. The backtracking stands out even more in *DS* games, in which the more focused level design and the unavailability of fast travel for most of *DS1* encourage players to revisit locations multiple times to keep tabs on particular NPCs. Moreover, in *ER*, the map helps the player track already discovered NPCs (though it doesn't predict where the NPCs will end up); *DS* players, by contrast, need to remember or note down the NPCs' locations, because no map is available in these games. The NPCs' erratic movements introduce another discontinuity between the topographic space (which normally creates an expectation of stability and reliable positioning of game elements) and the operational space of the player's exploration. Of course, after getting the hang of this system, players will come to expect the NPCs to move after a while, and seasoned Soulsring players may well remember the locations from previous playthroughs. However, an impression of instability is likely to linger and tinge the experience of even the most practiced player. Like the mixed affect of the atmosphere, the way in which the positioning of the NPCs changes to reflect the player's progress forms a unique aspect of the environmental storytelling of these games. It suggests that space itself isn't a stable (topographic) backdrop to the player's interactions, but rather a differentiated domain that is dynamically involved in a complex narrative.

***

Not only is space a central dimension of video games, as has been recognized by many scholars, but it can help achieve close integration between gameplay and narrative meaning making. As a design choice, environmental storytelling aims to embed narrative-advancing cues within the domain of the player's ludic interactions, without the jarring discontinuities that occur when gameplay-focused and narrative-focused sequences are simply chained together. This is the main takeaway of Jenkins's notion of environmental storytelling, which this chapter has refined by introducing a distinction between media-based and indexical spatial stories: the former involve semiotic artifacts such as letters or video clips directly available within the game world, while the latter use non-semiotic clues such as tracks and other physical marks.

Yet the fact that environmental storytelling can reduce discontinuities in the player's experience does not mean that discontinuities have no place in a game's narrative environment. On the contrary, gaps and tensions within the topographic, operational, and presentational dimensions of game spaces can help bring about certain aesthetic effects. In Soulsring games, discrepancies are a major component of the environmental storytelling, and they deepen the player's experience of literary complexity. The games' extensive item descriptions recall the media-based type of environmental storytelling, but they deliberately depart from it by introducing an unattributed narrative voice that doesn't originate from the items themselves—and, more importantly, that appears to contradict itself in a number of instances. The games' affective atmosphere and itinerant NPCs function indexically: they resonate with and anticipate the more localized stories found in the games' various locations, or (in the case of the NPCs) their moving bodies serve as a physical stand-in for the player's progression within a quest line. But these spatial stories are, too, rich in gaps and discontinuities having to do with clashing affective expectations or the general sense of topographic instability that derives from the NPCs' roaming. In other words: not only are Soulsring games highly proficient in forms of environmental storytelling found in many other games, but they introduce variations and innovations that contribute to their stratification of meanings. In the next chapter, I will address another element of this complexity, mirroring the instability of the concept of the "human" as imagined by Soulsring games.

Notes

1 Wei, Bizzocchi, and Calvert build on Nitsche's (2008) discussion of game spaces to identify these spatial forms.

2 Manfred Jahn (1997) has described the roles of these top-down and bottom-up effects in literary reading.

3 "The past is amassed, aggregated, enrolled, mixed up, recirculated, unforgotten, or torn out. It is the exchange with things that gather the 'pasts' that is of importance

and not an orientation with respect to a measured and passing temporality" (Olsen et al. 2012, 145).

4 Thus, in a similar vein, Nitsche introduces the concept of "evocative narrative elements," which "can be anything and any situation encountered in a game world that is structured to support and possibly guide the player's comprehension" (2008, 37).

5 The term "indexical" is also part of Fernández-Vara's (2011) Peircean vocabulary.

6 In the eighteenth-century treatise *Laocoon* (1962), Gotthold Ephraim Lessing already remarked on this tendency under the heading of "pregnant moment," arguing that it is the main means of achieving narrativity within static art forms such as paintings or sculptures.

7 See, e.g., https://darksouls.fandom.com/wiki/Opening_(Dark_Souls) for the script of the *DS1* opening cutscene.

8 https://darksouls2.wiki.fextralife.com/Dragonrider+Soul.

9 For more on narrators in video games, see Thon (2014).

10 https://www.reddit.com/r/darksouls/comments/qgk6li/item_descriptions_contrary_to_dialogue_or/.

11 https://darksouls.wiki.fextralife.com/Watchtower+Basement+Key.

12 https://darksouls.wiki.fextralife.com/Havel%27s+Ring.

13 https://www.reddit.com/r/darksouls/comments/gl5h3a/the_item_descriptions_arent_necesarilly_true/.

14 I refer here to James Phelan's (2017, 99) account of narrative unreliability, which distinguishes between three "axes"—of factual information, of interpretation, and of evaluation—and therefore three ways in which narrators can be unreliable. The unreliability I am identifying in the *DS* item descriptions pertains primarily to the first axis.

15 See again https://www.reddit.com/r/darksouls/comments/gl5h3a/the_item_descriptions_arent_necesarilly_true/.

16 See also Welsh (2020, n. 2), who—in a response to Vella's (2015) earlier *DS* article—also acknowledges the unreliability of the item descriptions.

17 https://www.reddit.com/r/darksouls/comments/b2fcgj/dark_souls_atmosphere_was_truly_special/

18 https://eldenring.wiki.fextralife.com/Weeping+Peninsula.

3 Reimagining Humanity as Multiplicity

When you die, you come back, but you lose all of your humanity. You become "hollow," your skin shrivels to suggest the exhaustion of your humanness (see figure 3.1). You can still retrieve your humanity, though, if you manage to find (or fight) your way back to the location where you died and pick up the glowing orb containing, along with your "souls," what's left of your humanity. But even after successful retrieval you don't become human right away. Instead, you rush to a bonfire and perform a ritual named "reverse hollowing," which sacrifices a small part of your humanity so you can call yourself human again. But it gets more complicated: humanity is both an in-game, consumable item and a numerical character trait—or "stat," in-game jargon—displayed in the top left corner of the screen, next to the health bar.[1] As an item, humanity is an oblong silver shape vaguely reminiscent of the human body; it can be found by defeating certain bosses or enemies. Consuming these rare items increases the player-character's humanity level, which in turn grants them a number of benefits, such as poison resistance and a better chance of finding certain weapons in the game world. These are some of the strange mechanics that surround "humanity" in *DS1*. The system is designed to be obscure and convoluted. A user comments on the Fextralife website: "I've played through the game multiple times … never understood the whole 'humanity' thing. I've read through this page multiple times … still do not understand the whole 'humanity' thing."[2] Obfuscating the "humanity thing" is clearly a deliberate strategy on the part of the game designers. Its significance extends well beyond gameplay: this is a game that, as part of its ludic sublime of incomprehension (to lift again Vella's phrase), consistently muddles the definition and boundaries of the human.

The other Soulsring titles implement mechanics reminiscent of *DS1*'s humanity. *DS2* comes closest to the original game by including "human effigies" as a consumable item, but the fact that this is an "effigy"—and thus clearly presented as a material object—marks a departure from the puzzling vagueness of the original's "humanity." In lieu of humanity, *DS3* has "embers," *Elden Ring* "rune arcs," which are rare consumables that allow the player to perform certain actions (for instance, related to the multiplayer system) or gain special powers. Functionally, they are similar to *DS1*'s humanity,

DOI: 10.4324/9781032684024-4

Figure 3.1 The player-character in their "hollow" form in *Dark Souls 1*.

but they greatly reduce its complexity both on the level of gameplay (there is no humanity stat, for example) and on the level of interpretation. Nevertheless, these games extend and deepen *DS1*'s engagement with the concept of the human through a vast array of characters, situations, and mechanics that call into question standard definitions of humanness. As I argue in this chapter, Soulsring games integrate in their gameplay and perform many of the insights emerging from posthumanist philosophy. In a broad sense, posthumanism "responds to a relatively straightforward imperative to think beyond humanism, anthropomorphism and anthropocentrism" (Callus, Herbrechter, and Rossini 2014, 112). To quote another influential thinker in this area, Cary Wolfe, posthumanism opposes a culturally entrenched understanding of the human as "achieved by escaping or repressing not just its animal origins in nature, the biological, and the evolutionary, but more generally by transcending the bonds of materiality and embodiment altogether" (2010, xv). This view of the human as uncoupled from the material, biological body is distinctive of Western modernity and ingrained in the philosophy of humanism (with the Enlightenment representing a defining moment in this history). The dominant Western understanding of the human is also markedly hierarchical and exclusionary: individuals belonging to certain privileged groups (white, male, cisgender, able-bodied, etc.) are prototypically aligned with humanness, with everyone else falling short of that ideal.

As formulated by Wolfe, Rosi Braidotti (2013), and the advocates of "critical posthumanism" (Callus, Herbrechter, and Rossini 2014), posthumanism dismantles the separation between the human subject and the material world and questions the hierarchies that are created by that separation. Foremost among these is the hierarchical relation between our species and the animal species with which we share a rich evolutionary history as well as experiences of embodied affect and vulnerability.[3] But posthumanism also concerns itself with the material realities of the planet's ecology: it suggests that human communities are deeply intertwined—"enmeshed," in Timothy Morton's (2010) terminology—with ecological systems. This idea runs counter to a long history of seeing the human as metaphysically superior to and in charge of the nonhuman world. Lastly, but of course significantly in a discussion of video games, posthumanism foregrounds the power of digital technologies to question the autonomy of the human subject—an idea notably pursued by Katherine Hayles's (1999, 2017) scholarship. Artificial Intelligence, for example, both augments human cognition and threatens to dislodge its philosophical centrality by detecting patterns in vast amounts of information that human minds would not be able to take in.[4]

It is important to stress that posthumanism isn't a coherent philosophical position but rather a thicket of ideas that speak to the breakdowns and blind spots of humanism. Nevertheless, there is a great deal of common ground between the various strands of posthumanist thinking, and it is within this common ground that the present chapter situates Soulsring games. I will argue that the games enact a critique of what Braidotti calls the "unitary" human subject entrenched in the humanist tradition: instead, the posthumanist concept of humanity performed by Soulsring games is "relational" and "constituted in and by multiplicity" (Braidotti 2013, 49). Embracing this type of subjectivity involves a recognition of the intersections between human or human-like individuals and nonhuman beings who are also capable of a rich affective life, including joy and suffering. The multiplicity of the posthumanist subject doesn't collapse the distinction between humanness (in the biological sense) and nonhuman beings, but it is rather based on the acknowledgment of entanglement: human subjectivity isn't sealed off from the external world but porous and traversed by the nonhuman, from the bacteria in our gut to the animals and plants that ensure our subsistence.

This entanglement also raises specific ethical demands, which thinkers like Deborah Bird Rose (2011) and Donna Haraway (2015) encapsulate through the image of "kinship." As a type of relationality, kinship has roots in our shared evolutionary history and also points to the need to acknowledge nonhuman suffering (and other emotional states) as deeply bound up with our actions: "Ethics open us to interactive, world-making dramas of encounter that facilitate the capacity to live together in the long term" (Rose 2011, 140). These "dramas of encounter" can be rewarding, but they can also be unsettling in that, as Rose continues, "to live in the world, to live in connectivity, is always to be living in proximity to death as well as to life, to cause death as well as to nurture life" (2011, 166–7). The cycles of violence and rebirth of Soulsring games give expression to this entanglement between the anthropomorphic player-character and a vast range of nonhuman creatures around them. I will explore this posthumanist entanglement in the games by tracing the evolution of humanity (as an in-game item and mechanic) and the human figure more generally. But fully understanding the extent of Soulsring games' engagement with posthumanist philosophy requires positioning them vis-à-vis the more conventional imaginary of the human that is found across a broad range of role-playing games. That is the task of my first section. I will then turn to the humanity mechanic of *DS* games and discuss two representational and affective strategies that are deployed by *ER* to renegotiate humanness: metamorphosis and the grotesque.

Fantasies of the Human

"The racial logics which structure game worlds mean that shifting representations do not necessarily change Fantasy's habits of Whiteness, but can rather re-inscribe them in new forms," writes Helen Young (2015, 12) in a book on race in the fantasy genre. There is little doubt that fantasy fiction has largely been dominated by white Americans or Europeans on the level of both authors and audiences. As Young suggests here, "racial logics" are deeply embedded within fantasy worlds on a formal level as well: fantasy conventions tend to align races with specific psychological or physical features, an idea that carries troubling real-world implications. This is equally true for tabletop role-playing games like *Dungeons & Dragons*, which have been enormously influential for fantasy video games and have helped shape both the mechanics and the imaginary of the genre. *D&D*-style games, in both their tabletop and digital forms, tend to deploy a specific understanding of race: at the start of the game, the player creates a character by choosing a race from a list that typically includes humans, orcs, elves, and so on. While the discourse of race is displaced here to what might be more accurately called different "species," these categories frequently embody stereotypes that are racial in a more conventional sense—with orcs, for example, serving as a monstrous counterpart to humans that taps into many of the clichés of Blackness (see Young 2015, chap. 4). In some instances, this choice of racial background even influences the character's abilities, stats, as well as moral alignment, a system that has attracted a great deal of criticism lately (D'Anastasio 2021).

Even when racial background doesn't define the character's skills or personality, it is a choice that players almost never get to revise in the course of gameplay: fantasy races thus tend to function as rigid identity categories that leave very little room for the multiplicity of the posthumanist subject as discussed by Braidotti. Surely, *D&D* manuals allow for races such as half-elves or half-orcs, which are of mixed ancestry (human and nonhuman), but these hybrid categories don't go very far in questioning the unitary quality of fantasy races; on the contrary, they presuppose and thus indirectly reinforce separation. Humanity, in particular, is seen in essentializing terms, as uncoupled from the nonhuman. It remains problematically close to images of whiteness, and thus also to the humanist notions that have come under intense scrutiny in posthumanist thinking.[5]

Soulsring games adopt a profoundly different approach to the imagination of humanness. While the available player-characters are visibly humanoid, there is no choice of race at the start of the games. Instead, *DS* players gradually realize that the protagonist's identity fluctuates between two poles that remain vague and undefined, entangled as they are with the games' cryptic lore: namely, being undead and hollowing. *DS1* starts in a location named Undead Asylum, a prison for individuals affected by the curse of Undeath, which condemns the player-character (and other similar beings) to endless cycles of death and resurrection. This is also the justification for the distinctive *DS* gameplay loop (see chapter 1). As the game's lore suggests, the more frequently an undead being dies, the closer they come to a state known as "being hollow," which refers to loss of free will and transformation into one of the zombie-like, mindless creatures the protagonist faces in the course of a playthrough. Yet, on the level of gameplay, the curse of Undeath that affects the player-character (and the hollowing that results from it) can always be reversed, at least until the next death.

Before detailing the mechanics of hollowing in *DS* games, it is worth remarking on how this setup challenges not only the racial determinism of the fantasy genre but also the conventions that surround the figure of the zombie in horror fiction and video games. A myth with roots in Haitian folklore, the zombie has been appropriated and transformed by countless representations across a wide range of media, with Hollywood films playing a major role in cultivating its imaginary.[6] Zombies are ontologically counterintuitive figures in that they challenge the basic distinction between death (they have corpse-like features) and aliveness (they display animacy by moving and acting in certain ways). Further complicating their ontological status, zombies are usually thought of as mindless and incapable of conscious experience, a deprivation expressed by *DS* games through the "hollowing" metaphor. As Sarah Juliet Lauro and Karen Embry put it, "the zombie is an antisubject, and the zombie horde is a swarm where no trace of the individual remains" (2008, 89). If the internal ontology of the zombie blurs a number of conceptual boundaries, the *external* distinction between zombies and humans tends to be rigid and clear-cut: in the vast majority of cultural representations involving zombies, humanity and zombies are starkly and dichotomously opposed. Similarly, whether it is started by a supernatural event or by a pathogen, in most cultural representations the process of zombification cannot be reversed: the zombie's former human subjectivity can almost never be restored. In that respect, despite Lauro and Christie's insistence that the zombie is "an apt icon for the post-human" (2011, 2), the zombie's dualistic distinction from "genuine" humanness works against the grain of the posthumanist subject, with its investment in multiplicity and openness. In *DS* games, by contrast, the player-character's status as an undead being doesn't cut them off from humanity altogether or turn them into "antisubjects": instead, they remain relationally bound up with the human even as the frequency of in-game death deepens their hollowing.

Fluctuating Humanity

DS games offer a visual indication of hollowing whenever the player opens the protagonist's profile: the more frequently they die, the more shriveled their facial features look (see again figure 3.1). There is in principle no limit to hollowing: no matter how many times the player-character dies, we remain in control and are given another chance to progress the game. (This is in contrast to some "roguelike" games, in which under certain conditions the player-character dies for good, forcing the player to restart from scratch.) However, the player typically experiences a number of disadvantages if they are in hollow form. For instance, in *DS1* hollow player-characters cannot summon other NPCs for important boss fights, which has a major impact on the game's overall difficulty level. In *DS2*, the player-character's health pool is reduced by 5% increments every time they die (and therefore advance their hollowing), up to a very significant 50% of their total health. *DS3* is the outlier in this respect, since the hollowing mechanic has no effect on gameplay but unlocks certain interactions and quest lines: here hollowing actually confers a narrative *advantage* in that it allows the player to reach one of the game's most interesting endings.

The hollowing process can be reversed, and this is where the item known as humanity comes into play in *DS1*: by burning humanity at a bonfire, *DS1* players can temporarily return to their original form—until of course they die again. (*DS2* uses Human Effigies for the same purpose, whereas *DS3* has Purging Stones.) Symbolically, this mechanic suggests that humanity isn't an intrinsic feature of the subject but requires constant maintenance work and even sacrifice.[7] *DS1* further complicates this mechanic by introducing a distinction between "solid" and "liquid" humanity, as the two types are known in the *DS* community.[8] The former refers to humanity as an item that can be collected from certain enemies (I will return to the nature of these enemies soon) and used to reverse hollowing. This type of humanity is solid because, if unconsumed, it stays in the player-character's inventory upon death. Liquid humanity, by contrast, is a metric shown by the game's interface—a level reflecting the number of humanity items the player has consumed since their last death. The higher this number, the more benefits the player receives, for instance in terms of poison resistance or "item discovery" (the likelihood of enemies dropping certain rare items). When the player dies, though, this humanity level drops to zero (because the player is undergoing hollowing) unless they are able to retrieve the lost humanity at their place of death. If they die a second time before retrieving it, the humanity will be completely lost along with whatever souls the player-character carried upon death. In the case of successful retrieval, the player is required to sacrifice a humanity level in order to reverse the hollowing: thus, for example, if a player dies with 11 humanity and manages to retrieve it, their level will decrease to 10.

These complicated and potentially confusing mechanics position humanity as both an item and an unstable, relational property within the game world: unlike traditional role-playing games, being human is no straightforward identity category in *DS*. Thus, although one may assume that consuming humanity (the in-game item) reverses hollowing in the sense of restoring the player-character's humanity (as a stable identity), this reading is repeatedly contradicted by the games. Instead, the player-character's baseline form is that of an undead creature, a figure that taps into well-known horror tropes such as the zombie but also subverts them by avoiding a strict human-zombie dichotomy. Crucially, then, the games stop short of assigning unambiguous humanity to the player. Far from being a race in the sense of many role-playing games, humanness turns into a relational property emerging from the mechanics of undeath and hollowing—and of course from their thematic and narrative significance as well.

In *DS1*, the relational nature of humanity is underscored by the *sources* of its "solid," consumable version. Since being human grants a number of benefits to the player and there is a chance of losing humanity upon death (if the player dies twice in a row), humanity items are one of the most valuable finds because they allow the player to counteract hollowing. While solid humanity is dropped by certain enemies, defeating humanoid creatures (such as bosses) only yields one humanity per playthrough, which is insufficient to meet the player's needs given the frequency of death and the ever-present possibility of humanity loss. Instead, the best method for collecting large amounts of humanity ("farming," in gaming terminology) requires killing beings that are clearly coded as nonhuman. My favorite farming route, for example, involved clearing all the rats near the Depths bonfire, then running back to the bonfire to reset the enemies and restart the cycle. The blue octopus-like creatures in the Duke's Archives can also drop humanity items. The irony is inescapable here: far from being an essential quality of the anthropomorphic player-character, humanity can be obtained by killing enemies that are markedly nonhuman and animal-like in shape. Humanness is thus presented as relational, as arising in the interstice between one being and another. In the world of *DS*, violence is our main means of acquiring humanity, but the starkness of that imagination of relations is tempered by the fact that (for the player-character, and for the creatures they defeat) death is never permanent: cycles of death and resurrection are needed to preserve a glimmer of humanness against the hollowing. Instead of affirming the superiority of the (human-like) player-character over nonhuman enemies, violence reveals what the protagonist and the rest of the game world share: namely, their being implicated in a constant renegotiation of both the life versus nonlife and the human versus nonhuman binary.

It is perhaps not too far-fetched to invoke anthropologist Eduardo Viveiros de Castro's work on Amerindian ontologies in this context: as Viveiros de

Castro argues, Amazonian cultures don't see humanity as something that developed and separated itself from animality through an evolutionary process, but rather as a shared substrate of human beings and nonhuman animals. In Viveiros de Castro's words: "For Amazonian peoples, *the original common condition of both humans and animals is not animality but, rather, humanity*" (2004, 465; emphasis in the original). Without of course claiming a direct link between *DS1* and Amerindian culture, it can be argued that the rat- or octopus-provided "humanity" of the FromSoftware game enacts a structurally similar vision of human–nonhuman relations: while distant from an anthropomorphic appearance, these creatures enable the player-character to extend their humanness, at least until their next death, because these game animals also participate in human nature. In line with posthumanist philosophy, the human subject is thus revealed to be relational, interstitial, and multiple in its physical embodiments.

Turning now to *ER*, that game does not have an explicit hollowing mechanic or humanity items. Narratively speaking, however, the player-character's identity as a Tarnished fulfills a similar role: at the start of the game, we are told (in the usual oblique fashion) that the protagonist belongs to a group of "tarnished" beings who fell from grace and were only allowed to re-enter the Lands Between after a catastrophic event known as the Shattering. "Arise now, ye Tarnished. Ye dead, who yet live. The call of long-lost grace speaks to us all," states the game's intro sequence, which aligns the Tarnished with what *DS* games had called "the undead." Nowhere in the game are the Tarnished explicitly described as human beings, which suggests that humanity in *ER* is no stable identity but rather a relational quality negotiated by players through their interpretation of the game, despite being less straightforwardly baked into gameplay than in *DS*. The fact that a Reddit user can ask "What counts as 'human' in the world of *Elden Ring*?," for instance, suggests that humanness isn't a given in the Lands Between, but a property hovering ambiguously between the player-character and the other enemies and NPCs we encounter during a playthrough.[9]

Functionally, however, the "grace" that emanates from the Erdtree and guides players throughout the game is analogous to humanity in *DS* games: as some commentators have noted, the flame hovering on the sites of grace scattered throughout the Lands Between is even visually reminiscent of the anthropomorphic shape of humanity items in *DS1* (see Tyson 2022). Grace represents a more-than-human intelligence that remains uncoupled from individual bodies but drives those willing to follow its "guidance" (the arrows visible on the map). Similar to the hollowing-humanity fluctuations of *DS*, grace serves as a foil to the decay visible on so many levels in the Lands Between—starting, of course, from the player-character's Tarnished status. From a gameplay perspective, however, the in-game equivalent of humanity items are the "Rune Arcs" (fragments of the shattered Elden Ring) that are used to activate Great Runes collected from some of the game's major bosses. When activated, these Great Runes grant benefits to the player, much like the human status in *DS* games. Despite the close resemblance between these mechanics and hollowing/humanity in *DS*, the posthumanist dimension of *ER* comes through most clearly from the motifs of metamorphosis and the grotesque, to which I turn in the next sections.

Boc's Metamorphoses

Drawing on Pascal Boyer's (2002) cognitive account of religion, Lisa Zunshine (2008) examines a wide range of narratives that build on "counter-ontological" objects and events—that is, objects and events that resist or challenge the ontological categories underpinning a certain culture.[10] Ontology in this cognitive sense refers to "the basic categories of existence, such as conscious beings, plants, nonliving inanimate objects, and events" (M. H. Kelly and Keil 1985, 405). For example, a zombie, as discussed previously, is a counterontological entity in that it combines features of death and animacy, thus violating the basic distinction between life and nonlife. One of the main pathways through which stories can challenge dominant ontologies is through metamorphosis, with human bodies transforming into nonhuman entities (or, more rarely, vice versa).

Ovid's *Metamorphoses*, a first-century poetic retelling of Greco-Roman mythology, has been hailed as an early articulation of posthumanism: it demonstrates a fluid ontology based on the constant "transformation of human beings into non-human, or at least non-anthropomorphic creatures" (Sissa 2019, 159). Also acknowledging the significance of Ovid's legacy, Bruce Clarke (2008) distinguishes between the metamorphic trope in premodern literature, including Ovid, and its iterations in the twentieth and twenty-first centuries. Premodern metamorphosis, for Clarke, tends to be more conceptually restrained, since the transformed body is eventually reinscribed "into the organic order (Daphne into a laurel tree, Narcissus into a flower) or returned to human status after a bestial detour" (2008, 2). Ontological distinctions (such as human versus plant or animal life) are thus temporarily destabilized but ultimately reaffirmed by the closed ending of a metamorphic sequence. More modern forms of metamorphosis, by contrast, produce "uncanny syntheses that retain transgressive stigmata and tend to refuse renaturalization" (Clarke 2008, 2). These uncanny metamorphoses speak to the multiplicity of the posthuman subject, in that they undermine the equation between subjectivity and a human (or human-like) body: instead, they present humanness as a property arising from the dynamically evolving relation between bodies of many different shapes.[11]

In *ER*, the clearest illustration of the posthumanist potential of metamorphosis comes from the quest line revolving around a character named Boc the Seamster. Early on in the game, when the player is exploring the area southeast of the Gatefront Ruins in Limgrave, they suddenly hear a voice calling out to them. The voice seems to come from a thicket of trees in the vicinity: it appears to have no discernible human source, but players may notice that it is at its loudest near a shrub. When attacked by the player, the plant immediately turns into a monkey-like creature, who remarks: "Ow! What'd you go and do that for! Hm? Oh, yes, I remember. Some clod turned me into a tree. You were just breaking the spell, weren't you. Thank you. The name's Boc." The Ovidian inspiration for this scene should be clear: an apt parallel is the nymph Daphne, who is metamorphosed into a laurel tree by her father while attempting to escape Apollo's sexual advances. But perhaps even more relevant here is the metamorphosis narrated by Dante in Canto XIII of the *Inferno*, which takes place in the wood of suicides. Hearing voices coming from the thicket, Dante initially assumes that people are hiding among the trees, but Virgil, his guide, reveals the truth by encouraging him to break off a twig from one of the shrubs:

> I think perhaps he [Virgil] thought that I was thinking
> those cries rose from among the twisted roots
> through which the spirits of the damned were slinking
>
> to hide from us. Therefore my Master said:
> "If you break off a twig, what you will learn
> will drive what you are thinking from your head."
>
> Puzzled, I raised my hand a bit and slowly
> broke off a branchlet from an enormous thorn:
> and the great trunk of it cried: "Why do you break me?"
>
> (2003, 105)

The puzzlement experienced by Dante in this scene is strikingly reminiscent of the player's surprise at the transformation of the tree into a speaking monkey in *ER*. In both cases, the encounter is initiated by an act of involuntary violence: the player attacking or bumping into the bush, in the FromSoftware game, Dante plucking a twig, in the *Inferno*. Violence is of course pervasive in Soulsring worlds. However, because most enemies respawn every time the player dies, the act of killing them doesn't involve a definitive affirmation of mastery. Instead, it serves as a reminder of how life and death are profoundly interlinked and crisscross the ontological divide between human and nonhuman entities. The player's unwitting attack on Boc fulfills a similar function: it discloses an ontologically puzzling relation by provoking an expression of physical pain ("Ow! What'd you go and do that for!" corresponding to Dante's "Why do you break me?"). These remarks challenge an intuitive ontology based on the separation between the linguistic human subject and inert vegetal matter incapable of verbal expression. The responses thus reveal a common ground of humanity (in the sense of articulated, verbal subjectivity) hovering between the human and the nonhuman; this common ground is made apparent by metamorphosis. In Dante's *Inferno*, the metamorphosis involves a human soul (the courtier Pier della Vigna) being turned into a tree as punishment for his death by suicide. In *ER*, this metamorphosis is enacted before our eyes as the monkey-like Boc emerges from an unmarked shrub, but the transformation is also said to reverse a *previous* metamorphosis, whose details remain vague ("Some clod turned me into a tree").

Significant is also the fact that *ER* imagines a transformation that leaves the human on the sidelines (from animal life to plant, and back), even as Boc's voice strongly cues humanness. Far from being an intrinsic quality of bodies of a certain kind and shape, humanity is uncoupled from the human form (at least in visual terms) and distributed across various domains of the nonhuman world. *ER*'s interest in the counterontological permutations of humanity is deepened as Boc's quest line progresses. We find out that Boc is a seamster: if we retrieve the tools of his trade from a boss, he is willing to alter the player-character's armor for free. As with many NPCs in *ER*, we run into Boc a number of times as we travel through the Lands Between: his monkey-like appearance remains unchanged throughout these encounters, but his gentle personality becomes increasingly attached to the protagonist. In fact, repeatedly throughout his dialogue lines, Boc embodies a certain courteousness and humaneness of manners that stand out in the bleak world of *ER*.

After a number of interactions, however, the player is faced with a choice that bears directly on the metamorphosis motif (and, as we may soon realize, on the character's survival). Boc remarks: "In all honesty, what do you think of me? Am I fit to serve a lord such as you, in all my ugliness? Must I be reborn, no matter what ill fate awaits me?" He also brings up the fact that one of the *ER* bosses, Rennala, is capable of conferring a new body. This is a mechanic that the player can use to "respec" the player-character, reshuffling key attributes and even physical features; it involves giving Rennala a rare item named "larval tear."

However, complying with Boc's rebirth request triggers a surprising chain of events. Boc disappears from the last location where the player saw him and instead moves to Rennala's location in Raya Lucaria. The first time the player meets him there, Boc has finally been reborn into a human body; surprisingly, though, he cannot speak. As soon as the player reloads the area or leaves and returns, Boc dies and the quest line ends abruptly. This is a disturbing twist, since the player presumably thought they were *helping* Boc overcome what he perceived as ugliness by taking on a human form. Instead, metamorphosis into a human body causes loss of voice and therefore relationality, eventually leading to Boc's demise. Just as unintentional violence brought out Boc's humanness (when we attacked the shrub in Limgrave), an act of kindness unwittingly deprives him of his humanness. This suggests that, in *ER*, metamorphosis is a two-edged sword: it can rearrange ontological categories and reveal an articulate posthuman subjectivity that transcends the human form;

yet, when metamorphosis *imposes* a human form, it results in the collapse of subjectivity.

The only way to avoid this tragic outcome in our interactions with Boc is to show him a clay mask or "Prattling Pate" that, as we read in the item description, "emits a voice that says 'You're beautiful.'"[12] This "wistful fetish" (again, according to the item description) can be found far from Boc's location: it is up to players to figure out that they need it to dissuade Boc from his self-perception of ugliness, thus preventing his death and ensuring his survival in the game world. The Prattling Pate is another example of how *ER* envisions humanness beyond the human form—in this case, by lending a voice and narrative agency to an inanimate object.

The mask thus represents another embodiment of humanity as a relational quality tied to shifts between the ontological categories of the human, the animal, the vegetal, and the material. Some of these shifts involve actual, diegetic transformation: Boc's metamorphosis from animal to plant and then back to animal; or his short-lived metamorphosis into the human form if the player decides to give him a larval tear. Other shifts are merely imaginative: the human voice being attributed to Boc or to a clay sculpture. Like *DS*, *ER* thus refuses to provide players with a stable image of what counts as human in the game world: instead, humanity is caught up in a series of affective and dynamic transactions that involve the anthropomorphic protagonist as well as a number of nonhuman characters. Paradoxically, it is by *denying* the visual attributes of the human that humanity—in the sense of an articulate, lively (if multiple) subjectivity—is preserved. This posthuman relationality involves both care and violence, but—importantly—the consequences of these seemingly opposing stances remain shrouded in uncertainty: care (as when we help Boc overcome his ugliness) can result in loss of subjectivity, whereas violence (as when we attack an unmarked bush in the forest) can reveal the depth of connection. To return to Rose's posthuman ethics, "To live in the world, to live in connectivity, is always to be living in proximity to death as well as to life, to cause death as well as to nurture life" (2011, 166–7). *ER* highlights this uneasy proximity of life and death, care and violence, by muddling the player's ability to fully predict the consequences of their actions as they engage with humanity in its metamorphic, unstable form.

Grotesque Grafting

The metamorphosis motif in *ER* isn't the only instance of ontological categories being disrupted in Soulsring games: their investment in the experience and affective register of the grotesque performs an analogous function, which can be traced across *DS* games and *ER*. According to Noël Carroll, the grotesque works by subverting "our categorical expectations concerning the natural and ontological order" (2003, 298). István Czachesz (2009) develops Carroll's account by foregrounding the role of expectations surrounding human bodies in grotesque experiences—an idea first formulated by Mikhail Bakhtin (1984) in a reading of François Rabelais's works. For Czachesz, the grotesque arises at the intersection of two factors: the violation of everyday experience (i.e., what I have called so far counterontological entities and events) and the use of emotionally salient bodily imagery, particularly imagery that violates bodily boundaries. Counterontological elements produce puzzlement but also arouse interest, whereas the disruption of the body's shape and integrity elicits fear and disgust: together, puzzlement, interest, fear, and disgust coexist (to varying degrees) in grotesque experiences.

As an example, consider one of the bosses in *DS1*, the Gaping Dragon. As the name suggests, this is a large dragon with withered wings and a giant vertical maw taking up most of the dragon's torso. The maw looks like a ribcage, and the dragon's main attack involves rearing its chest and slamming it on the ground in a forward motion, so as to trap the player within the ribcage. This horrific creature is a jumble of various animals and body parts players will be familiar with through both the real-world and the fantasy genre: its style of movement falls somewhere between a lizard and an insect but with no visible head and a large mouth-like opening where the torso should be. The Gaping Dragon thus disrupts a basic ontology of the body of animate creatures, including more conventional fantasy representations of dragons. But through the maw-like torso that opens to reveal the creature's stomach, this figure also violates the physical boundaries of the body—that is, the separation between its (normally hidden) interior and external space. The Gaping Dragon is thus a prototypical instance of the grotesque in *DS1*, and it gives rise to a distinctive blend of fear, disgust, and perplexed fascination.

While there is nothing in the Gaping Dragon that overtly suggests a renegotiation of the human form, other creatures in Soulsring games combine grotesque and anthropomorphic elements. For example, the two "primordial serpents" of *DS1* (Kingseeker Frampt and Darkstalker Kaathe) are giant serpents with a large grin and whiskers reminiscent of a rabbit's floppy ears. They are not enemies but helpers, although in the course of the game the player is forced to side with either Frampt or Kaathe—a decision that unlocks different endings (see the discussion of the endings in chapter 6). Despite their grotesque appearance, the two serpents are also surprisingly articulate and courteous: in fact, their elaborate language is similar to Boc's in *ER* and falls into a long history of monstrous creatures capable of ornate expression (among them Frankenstein's monster in Mary Shelley's novel). This is, for example, how Frampt introduces himself: "I am the primordial serpent, Kingseeker Frampt, close friend of the Great Lord Gwyn. Chosen Undead, who has rung the Bell of Awakening. I wish to elucidate your fate. Do you seek such enlightenment?" The serpents' eloquence and benign tone are an indication of their latent humanness. Also significant is that the grotesqueness of Frampt and Kaathe is more endearing than repulsive: the fear they may initially inspire in the audience is modulated by their relatability and even cuteness, two affective features that invite players' acknowledgment of their humanness.[13] Yet the primordial serpents' motivations and contribution to the player-character's quest are never fully spelled out: despite Frampt's remark, his dialogue lines never truly "elucidate [the player-character's] fate." In that respect, Frampt and Kaathe embody a posthumanist subjectivity that includes but cannot be reduced to articulate human-like expression, because their identity and exact role in the game's cosmology elude straightforward explanation. The serpents thus simultaneously prompt and discourage attributions of humanness, calling for a mode of engagement that resonates with contemporary thinking on the need to radically alter our understanding of the subject as more-than-human.

In *DS2*, grotesqueness is blended with the human figure in one of the most haunting and mysterious characters of the game, the Embedded (see figure 3.2). On the top level of Drangleic Castle, the player comes across a metal door molded on an upside-down human body; a large keyhole is visible on the human figure's face. This is a counterontological representation, since it blends the human and the inanimate and also foregrounds the openness of the body in an incongruous way (through the mouth-keyhole mapping). The key can be found by killing one of the game's bosses, and its item description reads: "Plunge the key into the Embedded to bring a rhapsodic end to his fate. The once-human Embedded, realizing that he could never resist the temptation of the flesh, bound himself eternally with chains. Since then, he has awaited the day that somebody will find this key, and bury it within his bosom."[14] As the description announces, restoring the human form of the Embedded means condemning him to death, which is precisely what happens when we unlock the door. Similarly to Boc's deadly metamorphosis

Figure 3.2 Liberating the Embedded in *Dark Souls 2*.

into a human being, *freeing* the Embedded—an apparent act of care—actually brings about his demise. Restoring the human form, in Soulsring games, is a gesture associated with violence, even when violence isn't intended; on the other hand, violence is a mode of discovery that can reveal surprising (if grotesque) connections across the human–nonhuman divide.

The grotesque can also convey the breakdown of humanity and therefore of connection, though. In *ER*, seemingly anthropomorphic bosses are completely dehumanized to suggest the loss of the qualities associated with Boc and the serpents (articulateness, care, vulnerability, and so on). A striking example is provided by Godrick the Grafted, the boss players encounter when leaving the game's starting area, Limgrave. While seemingly human, Godrick has had numerous arms implanted ("grafted") onto his body, which create unique challenges in combat, since the player is forced to dodge swipes from multiple arms. When Godrick's health is down to around 50%, his second phase is introduced by a cutscene in which we see him cut off one of his arms and graft a dragon's head in its place. These are, of course, grotesque elements through the counterontological mixture of body parts (human and nonhuman) and the deliberate manipulation of the body's boundaries. Nor is Godrick an exception: grotesque bodily modifications are commonplace in the world of *ER*, and they include an array of multiarmed (or -legged) creatures such as the Grafted Scion and the Revenants. The Scion, for instance, has a recognizable human (even childlike) head resting on a tangle of human and nonhuman limbs.[15] If Boc and the primordial serpents in *DS1* evoke human feelings within seemingly nonhuman bodies, these disfigured human shapes create fear and disgust at the tragic *loss* of humanness: they are cruel, unidimensional characters that mark a sharp departure from Boc's complex positioning vis-à-vis the human–nonhuman distinction.

In sum, counterontological fantasies of distorted embodiment are responsible for complicating attributions of humanness in Soulsring games: anthropomorphic bodies are emptied out of their subjectivity, while seemingly nonhuman, grotesque bodies are endowed with human-like traits. In this way, humanity is both evoked and challenged by counterontological elements that speak to a posthumanist critique of the human versus nonhuman binary.

***

Posthumanist discussions on subjectivity aim to dislodge the idea of humanity from the dualistic thinking of Western modernity. This posthumanist view emphasizes that the human, far from being a biological given, is bound up with the nonhuman world and implicated in an exclusionary history of racism and sexism. Critical posthumanists (see, e.g., Callus, Herbrechter, and Rossini 2014) don't argue that the human should be discarded altogether, but that it should be opened up to denote relations that may involve nonhuman animals as well as inanimate entities: in at least some situations, these entities can also be described as partaking of humanity in an extended sense. The concepts of subjectivity and humanity thus intersect and transcend human experience understood narrowly, as a feature of certain biological bodies. One of the most lucid articulations of this posthumanist understanding is offered by Rose: "There is no predetermined essence of humanity, no ultimate goal toward which we are heading, and … we experience what appear to be astonishingly open ways of being and becoming human" (2011, 57). As I have argued in this chapter, Soulsring games afford insight into the openness of the human through their reshuffling of the tropes of fantasy and horror fiction. Instead of a stable human "race" that can be distinguished from other ways of being, they feature an anthropomorphic protagonist but refuse to characterize them as human in any overt way. Rather, the protagonist is caught in a dialectic of "undeath" and "hollowing" that in itself challenges the dichotomy, typical of horror fiction, between zombies (hollow beings, in *DS* terminology) and humans.

In *DS* games, and most notably in *DS1*, humanity exists both as a temporary status of the player-character and as an item that can be collected from certain enemies (including enemies that are anything but anthropomorphic). The sophisticated mechanics surrounding humanity make sure that the human is never a given, but rather a flexible, quality that is renegotiated every time the player-character dies. *ER* doesn't include a straightforward humanity mechanic but rather uses thematic and narrative elements to perform a similar redistribution of human qualities across the human–nonhuman divide. I have singled out metamorphosis and the grotesque as figures that are responsible for this rethinking of humanity along posthumanist lines in *ER*. In both instances, the counterontological work performed by metamorphic or grotesque representations undercuts the simplistic equation of humanity with human or human-like bodies. Rather than being a biological essence, humanity emerges from relations between human-like features (particularly, in my example, articulateness of verbal expression) and the nonhuman world. These relations are unstable and may, in some instances, leave out the human form completely, as in the case of Boc's metamorphoses, which come to a tragic end, unwittingly, when an anthropomorphic body is imposed on Boc by the player.

Whatever form this relational network takes in Soulsring games, it includes both care and violence, and the consequences of these stances are sometimes unpredictable: care can lead to the breakdown of subjectivity, as when we think we are advancing Boc's quest in *ER* by turning him into a human being, but in fact we are condemning him to death. By contrast, violence can lead to surprising encounters that expand subjectivity beyond the human. The grotesque itself is an ambiguous affective mode, suggesting both continuity between the human and the nonhuman and the tragic loss of humanity. The cycles of death and rebirth in which, in different ways, all Soulsring games engage contribute to bringing out the relationality of the human concept. The next chapter turns to how relationality is negotiated experientially through multiplayer interactions.

Notes

1 The original Japanese reads 人間性, "human nature."
2 https://darksouls.wiki.fextralife.com/Humanity.
3 See Anat Pick's (2011) work in animal studies on vulnerability as a shared experience across the human–animal divide.
4 For a survey of historical and conceptual overlaps between posthumanism and digital cultures, see Ciccoricco (2016).
5 Murray (2017, chap. 2) offers a comprehensive discussion of the aesthetics of whiteness in video games, although her examples don't include the fantasy genre.
6 See the collection edited by Christie and Lauro (2011) for a helpful overview of the zombie's historical evolution.
7 See this statement by a Reddit user: "When you think about it, consuming Humanity is cannibalism. Humanity is a part of a person, and you're devouring it in order to gain power." https://www.reddit.com/r/darksouls3/comments/5kky9w/the_lore_of_hollowing_and_humanity/.
8 See, e.g., https://darksouls.fandom.com/wiki/Humanity_(item) for this terminology.
9 https://www.reddit.com/r/Eldenring/comments/vf6ib8/what_counts_as_human_in_the_world_of_elden_ring/.
10 In Zunshine's words, "By failing to be assimilated by the category that it has initially activated—in this particular case, a living being, a person—a counterontological entity remains a promising source of new interpretations or, to make the same point somewhat differently, a fruitful source of new stories" (2008, 67).
11 For more on metamorphosis as a figure of the posthuman in contemporary fiction, see Caracciolo and Lambert (2019, 51–4).
12 https://eldenring.wiki.fextralife.com/Prattling+Pate+You're+Beautiful.
13 https://www.reddit.com/r/darksouls/comments/k6eaht/does_anyone_else_think_frampt_and_kaathe_are_cute/.
14 https://darksouls2.wiki.fextralife.com/Key+to+the+Embedded.
15 For a detailed description of the Grafted Scion, including its multiple body parts of human and nonhuman origin, see this video: https://youtu.be/B_RkJJMwfCA.

4 Community

Asynchronous Multiplayer and Shared Difficulty

Digital media and the internet have had a profound impact on the definition and practice of the collective. Politics routinely relies on the distributed network of social media, which creates unprecedented possibilities for collective organization but also new challenges for democratic processes, including AI-driven misinformation and interference.[1] For audiences of artistic or entertainment practices, the forms of the collective are changing as well. Fiction readers are increasingly using Goodreads.com or similar services to share impressions of the books they read, on social media-like platforms that are easily monetized by corporations such as Amazon (which owns Goodreads).[2] Online or "multiplayer" gaming represents a mode of collectivity that is even more fundamentally bound up with digital media and the internet. Combining play and narrative engagement in a shared, intersubjective context, online games are a microcosm illustrating many of the dilemmas that underlie digital communities—the promise of decentralized cooperation but also the ever-present threat of irresponsible or predatory behavior. This chapter focuses on how *ER* navigates those dilemmas through its innovative multiplayer environment, which builds on earlier *Dark Souls* (*DS*) titles while improving and deepening their collaborative systems.

Multiplayer video games can create intersubjective experiences in profoundly different ways. Players can share a physical space, for example when a game allows for "split-screen" multiplayer on the same computer or console system. More frequently today, though, multiplayer gaming involves sharing a virtual environment remotely, through an internet connection. It can span a broad spectrum from pure competition (a free-for-all "deathmatch," in which every player is fighting for themselves) to purely cooperative experiences (in which all players work together to achieve a certain goal). Team-based multiplayer games fall halfway on this spectrum: they combine competition (against the opposing team or teams) and cooperation (within the team). In most of these games, players act within the same simulated environment through the mediation of the player-character.

Across this range of multiplayer experiences, two features tend to remain constant in modern games. The first is that players have to be connected simultaneously to play together: as in real-life interaction, their player-characters

DOI: 10.4324/9781032684024-5

need to occupy the same digital environment synchronously to compete or collaborate. Second, players are allowed and even encouraged to communicate directly, either through in-game chat or by using external voice chat services such as Discord, to coordinate their actions. Soulsring games challenge both of these conventions by allowing for asynchronous multiplayer and by placing significant constraints on communication.[3] As I will argue in this chapter, this unusual way of bringing players together puts pressure on some of the stereotypes and assumptions surrounding gaming culture. Asynchronous gameplay and constrained communication are forms that enable responsible and critical practices in online communities, favoring the archaeological mindset I have already discussed as well as the sustained interpretive negotiations I will turn to in the next chapter.

Of course, correlating a certain form (in this case, two game mechanics) with an effect is always tricky: many factors shape the *DS* and *Elden Ring* (*ER*) community, and it is difficult to both generalize about a community and trace all of its features to the developers' design choices. It is also important not to idealize FromSoftware fans, who are certainly not immune to the problematic competitiveness that, as I will show, affects large swathes of contemporary gaming. "Git gud" ("get good"), for example, is a refrain that keeps popping up in FromSoftware discussions. Literally, it signals that the difficulty of Soulsring games can only be overcome through patience and hard work—that is, by gradually honing one's skills. That refrain is often used to disparage new players, or "casual" players, who don't reach (and, typically, don't aspire to reach) a high skill level.[4] Moreover, it is tempting to talk about the FromSoftware community in general terms, but the reality is that the community is split into at least two subgroups. Some players focus on the games' lore in their interactions, engaging in the type of "archaeological fandom" I discussed in chapter 2. By contrast, other players tend to value the combat more than the games' narratives, and it is in this group that the "git gud" motto tends to come up most frequently. This also reflects the fact that, as I mentioned, Soulsring games do have a synchronous multiplayer component enabling player-versus-player (PvP) encounters: these are duels in which players confront each other, often trying out different combinations of weapons and types or classes of player-character (collectively referred to as the player's "build"). The inherent competitiveness of this dueling practice goes hand in hand with the "trash talk" that, as we will see, plagues the world of online gaming, but this type of negative behavior in Soulsring games is certainly less widespread than in games that are more explicitly or exclusively geared toward PvP combat.

This difference has to do with the fact that the games' asynchronous multiplayer and constrained communication keep toxic behavior in check. These forms don't achieve that result on their own, of course: they are supported by the games' inherent difficulty level and also by their narrative complexity, both of which encourage teamwork. Community is also built into the games through a messaging system that empowers players to help each other out in making sense of challenging situations or obscure lore. This is perhaps most evident in lore-focused discussion groups, where (despite the occasional heated disagreement or controversy) players share and debate their interpretation of the games' environmental storytelling in constructive ways. Even in PvP-oriented gameplay, the impossibility of direct verbal interaction with other players results in a number of unwritten rules that are meant to keep PvP duels fair and civil.[5] Thus, asynchronous and constrained-communication multiplayer work together with other aspects of the games' design to foster more supportive forms of online collectivity than can be found elsewhere. Before turning to my discussion of community building in *ER*, a survey of work on uncooperativeness in online gaming will help me illustrate the type of behavior that Soulsring games are striving to minimize.

Toxic Behavior and "Grief" in Online Communities

Any generalization about a place as divided as the internet is of course bound to invite disagreement, but it seems safe to suggest that gaming communities, in general, have a rather poor track record when it comes to respectful behavior. The culture of hardcore gaming is strongly (if stereotypically) aligned with notions of hypercompetitive masculinity. Even if gaming audiences have become far more inclusive and diverse over the years, the controversies surrounding the "GamerGate" in 2014–15 demonstrate that sexist assumptions are still entrenched in at least some gaming communities.[6] The GamerGate was a harassment campaign launched by online commentators who targeted female developers, particularly well-known figures in the indie gaming industry whose games engage with issues of social justice or contemporary politics. Writing before the GamerGate, Mia Consalvo already noted "a pattern of a misogynistic gamer culture and patriarchal privilege attempting to (re)assert its position" (2012). While it would be unfair to see GamerGate advocates as representative of the "average" gamer, their response is symptomatic of larger rifts within the world of gaming, which can easily spiral into irresponsible or toxic behavior.

If we focus more narrowly on multiplayer interactions, problematic behavior is not hard to come by. A longitudinal study by Jesse Fox and Wai Yen Tang (2018) offers a comprehensive picture of players' experiences with the online game *Team Fortress 2*. Their point of departure is that "several studies have found negative social interaction to be common within online games … and more broadly in gamer culture" (2018, 4058). The results, based on diary observations by a relatively small number of participants (n = 38), broadly confirm this idea. Verbal aggression—in the form of teasing "trash talk" or downright harassment—is frequent, with around 76% of players reporting such behavior.[7] A player's perceived lack of skill is one of the main reasons for this kind of harassment. Toxic masculinity and sexism are two more themes emerging from the qualitative data.

A study by Jonas Heide Smith (2007) highlights two patterns that contribute to uncooperative behavior in multiplayer games even in the absence of direct verbal harassment: cheating and grief. The former means interacting with the game in a way that wasn't intended by the developers, usually by exploiting a coding error and in a way that gives the player an unfair advantage in competing against others. "Grief," by contrast, is gaming jargon for destructive behavior targeted at other players that doesn't result in any strategic advantage for the player performing it. In a survival game, for example, grief could involve destroying or damaging a structure built by another player just for the sake of bullying them. For Smith, the frequency of cheating and grief in online gameplay places severe limitations on multiplayer collaboration. These behavioral patterns introduce intersubjective tensions and dilemmas that potentially destabilize online communities. Smith understands these destabilizing forces through the lens of the concept of the "tragedy of the commons," which was first introduced by ecologist Garrett Hardin (1968) and later picked up by many economists. In essence, the tragedy has to do with how, if left unregulated, shared resources are bound to be exploited by one individual or group acting out of self-interest. In the case of multiplayer games, of course, resources are rarely finite in an absolute sense: even if an online world runs out of a particular material, it is always possible to reset or restart the game.[8] The "tragedy" of online gaming thus has more to do with social capital than with resource usage, with harassment, cheating, and grief being the most significant challenges to cooperation and fair competition in multiplayer contexts.

The answer, as Smith highlights, is more regulation—and indeed that is what asynchronous and constrained-communication multiplayer provide. But before I expand on those elements in *Elden Ring*, it is worth stressing that toxic or uncooperative in-game behavior (that is, during gameplay) frequently translates into unsupportive or hypercompetitive online communities: the "trash talk" that plagues multiplayer game experiences spills over into Reddit threads, YouTube comments, and so on. Obviously, the link between in-game behavior and the larger collectives built around games isn't always straightforward; but in the case of *ER* and other Soulsring titles there is a clear connection between the two, as we will see in the next section.

Forms of Community Building in *Elden Ring*

As I noted several times, playing Soulsring games can be a deeply frustrating experience: YouTube is full of "rage quit" videos with players abandoning a FromSoftware game after failing to beat a boss by just a handful of health points after countless attempts. In part, the frustration is relieved by the games' focus on community building, which is realized through a number of sophisticated multiplayer systems. While my focus is on asynchronous multiplayer here, it is important to note that *DS* games and *ER* also feature synchronous multiplayer, which comes in two flavors: player-versus-player (PvP) encounters or cooperative exploration and player-versus-environment (PvE) combat. Like everything else in FromSoftware games, this synchronous multiplayer doesn't follow the conventions of most multiplayer games. There is no "match-making" menu where we can easily find co-players here, no way of simply inviting a friend to our game world with one mouse click. Instead, synchronous multiplayer entails using a complicated series of in-game items. For example, in *ER*, an object called "Small Golden Effigy" is required for cooperative multiplayer, whereas the red equivalent is for PvP. These items can be used anywhere in-game, but activating an effigy near a statue called "Effigy of the Martyr" will increase the chances of summoning another player. If we want to enlist another player to help us fight against a tough boss (PvE), we need to consume another item, called "Furlcalling Finger Remedy." None of these items are available from the start of the game: we need to find them through single-player gameplay.

Given these complicated subsystems, one would expect a clear explanation of what each item does, but (as we know from previous chapters) this is a game that steers away from any form of hand-holding: instead, players are left to figure out how the multiplayer mechanics work by themselves—or, more likely, they will need to look up a guide on the internet.[9] This is the first way in which *ER* builds a strong connection between in-game experience and a larger community of players: its gameplay workings and narrative are so murky that the player is essentially required to use internet resources to make the most of the game—and, indeed, community-maintained websites provide extremely detailed information not just on how the multiplayer systems work but also on the location of special items, secret doors or passageways, and so on. Of course, discussion fora and online guides exist for many if not most games; but in the vast majority of these games, a reasonably competent player can get away without using those resources systematically: in *ER*, by contrast, one is likely to miss a significant number of in-game encounters and experiences without engaging with the community.

The game's inherent difficulty plays a central role in the discourse produced by the community. Difficulty here covers every single aspect of the game, from the extreme challenge posed by the boss fights to the intricate narrative universe and the arcane gameplay mechanics. Virtually all of these dimensions of the game invite players to pay attention to what other members of the community are saying or writing. The result, as I mentioned, is a close integration between gameplay and resources that are external to game experience. This integration also leads to a collaborative culture that is unparalleled in other areas of contemporary gaming. In an informal survey I ran on Reddit in September 2022, 42 players were asked: "How would you characterize the internet community surrounding *Dark Souls* games and *Elden Ring*? Include one or more keywords." Words such as "helpful" or "supportive" were used by 20 of the respondents. Only seven respondents expressed more negative feelings, with some of them complaining about the "elitism" of those who routinely disparage other players' lack of skill, typically under the infamous "git gud" rubric.[10] "Git gud" ("get good") signals that hard work is required to master the game's systems; in practice, that slogan is often used to harass newcomers to Soulsring games. It is a way of suggesting that new players don't have what it takes to tackle the challenge.

In this respect, the FromSoftware community is afflicted by many of the problems noted in the previous section. Historically, it has been split into two camps: some groups focus on competitive multiplayer (PvP), while others foreground the games' complex backstories (the lore-hunting community). Disparaging or toxic behavior is of course more widespread in the PvP community due to its inherent competitiveness. The strategies I will discuss in the next two sections—asynchronous multiplayer and constrained messaging—define the baseline experience of *ER* and will therefore shape players' engagement regardless of whether they are more invested in PvP or in the game's lore. While the strategies cannot completely prevent problematic behavior, they tilt the balance toward more supportive interactions than are found in other areas of contemporary gaming.

Largely, the Soulsring community defines its identity in opposition to the inherent difficulty of the games. That setup creates a sense of camaraderie that (as we will see) favors cooperation or at least mutual respect even in competitive, PvP-oriented gameplay. That effect is magnified by the fact that, during gameplay, our interactions are severely constrained by the messaging system, which leaves little room for disparaging comments. Instead, the already mentioned integration of in-game experience and internet commentary is designed to maximize more constructive interactions, as exemplified by the sophistication of lore-centric discussions (the topic of the next chapter).

Bloodstains and Ghosts

ER is unlike most other games in that it doesn't draw a clear distinction between single-player and multiplayer mode at the level of the menu interface. Instead, a multiplayer session can only be started within the world of a "solo" playthrough. But the boundary between game modes is also blurred by the asynchronous elements, traces, or echoes of other players' worlds that are visible, as long as the player is connected to the internet, even if they are not actively seeking multiplayer experiences. These asynchronous elements fall into two categories: bloodstains and white ghosts. When I enter a new area and notice a large number of bloodstains on the ground, I know that I am about to face a difficult boss or group of enemies. Interacting with the bloodstains shows me how a fellow player died: the player enters my world as a red ghost, immortalized for just a few seconds at the time of their death. The process that governs the appearance of bloodstains is algorithmic and inscrutable, but it can provide me with valuable information on how to survive the next encounter. When I find a cluster of bloodstains near a drop, for example, I know that the fall isn't survivable, and I look for another spot to climb down. More importantly, though, the bloodstains are a tangible trace of the difficulty of the game, they suggest that my struggle with the game's infuriatingly hard bosses is no exception—not merely the result of my lack of skill—but rather a shared experience. Implicitly, then, these physical marks situate my potential frustration within a larger pattern of collective endeavor, which partly alleviates such frustration.

In addition to the bloodstains, while I explore the sprawling world of *ER* I come across ghostly shapes that move, jump, and fight in much the same way as I do. I am unable to interact with these ghosts directly; in fact, they vanish after a few seconds. It is unclear whether these ghostly sequences are prerecorded from other players' playthroughs or live snippets from another user's gameplay. But the difference is inconsequential, because no direct interaction is possible: I can see other players' ghosts, but they cannot see me. As a player on Reddit puts it, "I honestly love the Ghosts, even if it's not in real-time, it makes such a deadly world feel less depressing knowing there are others adventuring alongside you."[11] Another player on the same subreddit ventures an explanation in terms of the game's lore, with a reference to the *DS* series (where ghosts work in much the same way): "Since before you fulfill one of the prophecies and become the Chosen Undead, it basically meant that any single Undead could one day be the Chosen one, meaning up to the point of accomplishing it, you may have failed and someone else took your place in a different instance in the future, as well as those who did it in the past." Just as the game's backstories are arranged on a multitude of temporal planes, these ghosts—the red ones accessed through bloodstains and the white ones that appear on my screen from time to time—evoke a long history of struggles against the game's difficulty: they involve me in a community that, while not physically present while I play, supports my efforts by showing that many others have tried, failed, and presumably succeeded in the end. Even when I am not engaged in online gameplay, the *ER* community maintains a ghostly, benign presence in my game world.

"Praise the Message"

The messages left by other players on the ground go even further. In *DS2*, a character asks the player early on in the game: "Did you notice any letters on the ground on the way here? These are messages that have jumped the fissures between worlds .... If your will to soldier on falters, try leaving a message. Somebody out there is sure to listen." In *ER*, too, my game world is strewn with glowing markers on the ground or floor of the locations I visit: when I interact with them, a message pops up on my screen. I can rate these messages as "good" or "poor" depending on their usefulness or emotional value. I can leave a message for other players, too, and my health bar is topped up every time another player likes one of my messages. This is asynchronous communication, since there is always a delay between the creation of a message and its appearance in another player's world; whether that happens or not depends (like the ghosts discussed in the previous section) on the game's algorithm. But the messages are also a *constrained* form of communication, in that I cannot type a message directly but I have to pick from a word list and arrange the terms within a fixed syntax. The templates include "Praise the ...", "Why is it always ...?", or "... ahead," while the word list covers basic actions (attacking, healing, etc.), situations (battle, hiding place, danger, etc.), places (cave, river, etc.), and so on. These constraints ensure full interoperability of the messages across languages, because my text in English will appear in (for example) German or Japanese to those who are playing the German or Japanese version of the game. The constrained nature of the messages limits questionable behavior including hate speech or trash talk directed at other players; but it also poses a creative challenge, in that players are asked to work with the fixed syntax and limited word list to convey meaning.

Some of these meanings are practical and serve as in-game advice: just before entering a room, for example, I may come across a message saying "Group ahead," which tells me that I have to heal up and prepare for a tough fight. Other messages provide clues for some of the game's most difficult puzzles, which would otherwise be difficult to solve without using an online guide or walkthrough (unless the player has hours to spend on trials and errors).[12] Thanks to the messages, I don't need to quit the game and consult internet resources; I can simply follow the advice provided by other players in-game. Due to the constrained nature of the messages, solving the puzzle will still require some guesswork, because the other players cannot tell me what to do in plain language. Thus, the messages are unlike a step-by-step walkthrough in that they don't completely spoil the pleasure of discovery, they just gently nudge the players toward the solution. Effectively, this system builds into the game world the community advice one would normally find outside of the game itself, on specialized websites or discussion groups. But it does so in a way that preserves immersion and also doesn't completely take agency away from the player.

Moreover, the messages are not purely utilitarian. When I emerge from a difficult boss fight at the end of Stormveil Castle, I find myself on a hill overlooking Liurnia of the Lakes. The view from this clifftop is striking, with rocky outcrops dotting the lakes and the spires of a far-off town shrouded in mist (see figure 2.1). It wouldn't be far-fetched to see this panorama as a reference to Caspar David Friedrich's quintessentially Romantic painting, *Wanderer above the Sea of Fog*: after all, this game brims with allusions to European art history. While I admire the sublime landscape of Liurnia I notice a message on the ground, which tells me in simple words: "Gorgeous view."

This, of course, doesn't add anything to my technical understanding of the game, but it does enhance my experience of *ER* through a sense of sharing this sublime feeling with the community. In other instances, the intersubjective sharing enabled by the messaging system relates to the more grueling aspects of the game. A comment on a YouTube video essay on *DS* games reads as follows: "You know what makes me happy about these games? When I defeat a boss after hours of trying and I read the messages on the floor saying 'I did it' or 'good job' it makes me feel like I am part of a group that struggled together and made it through."[13] The messages build community in the absence of direct interaction; in a sense, it is the loneliness of "solo" gameplay—the hours and hours spent learning the patterns of a single enemy—that amplifies the emotional resonance of these words.

Of course, not all messages are meant in earnest: some are deliberately misleading ("hidden passage here" where there is no hidden passage), and some are humorously self-referential ("by the way, praise the message"). After a boss fight in which we confront our own doppelganger (a "mimic tear"), a player reportedly came across the following message: "didn't expect weak foe, therefore time for introspection."[14] With some experience of the game, even the most bizarre or misleading of these messages becomes an in-joke, a quip that creates bridges across worlds and players' experiences. Through asynchronous gameplay and constrained communication, *ER* succeeds in building a community that is supportive both practically and emotionally. Perhaps the conclusion of a game journalist, Rebekah Valentine, isn't too idealized, then: "With a community dedicated to earnest, altruistic information exchange, a lack of feedback for misinformation and trolling, and no real direct way to bother other players who don't want to be bothered, *Elden Ring* has established an information system that can, by and large, be trusted. What other social network can say that in 2022?" (Valentine 2022). In no small part, that success is due to the game's combination of two factors: the complexity of its multiplayer, which weaves together single-player experience and community building; and the game's unusually high difficulty level, which can only be mastered through intersubjective sharing of both information and emotional resources.

***

In today's digital world, the definition of community straddles real-life intersubjectivity and the possibilities offered by digital communication. This chapter has offered a case study on community building in the context of multiplayer gaming, focusing on the affordances of two mechanics that defamiliarize the conventions of online gaming: asynchronous multiplayer, which enables interaction across a spatiotemporal gap, and constrained communication. As Smith (2007) argues, multiplayer games are afflicted by a version of the "tragedy of the commons": selfish behavior is the norm unless there are checks and balances in place that make such behavior costly. In online gameplay, players frequently engage in irresponsible or antisocial actions such as cheating or harassing other players—a trend that mirrors the toxicity of hardcore gaming culture. *ER* and other FromSoftware games implement mechanics that are aimed at reducing this toxicity and creating a supportive gaming environment. This feat becomes even more remarkable if we consider the inherent difficulty and complexity of these games, which do not spoon-feed the player but rather present them with worlds full of mystery and intricate systems. These are literary games, to use again Ensslin's (2014) terminology, that reward patience and attention to detail. The more complex the game, the more the community is asked to fill in the gaps by explicating basic mechanics, reconstructing the narrative and its implications, and elaborating on the rich mythology or lore of these universes. Reconstruction and elaboration are typically communal interpretive activities, as I will explore in more detail in the next chapter. The considerable level of nuance and sophistication of discussions in the Soulsring community is due to many factors, but important among them are the design decisions that steer players toward certain kinds of interaction: both the asynchronous multiplayer elements (the ghosts) and the messaging system immerse gamers in an intersubjective world of shared joys and frustrations—a system that tends to discourage irresponsible behavior. The takeaway here, also beyond the world of gaming, is that more responsible forms of online togetherness can be cultivated through innovative formal design: that is, by adopting strategies that reward collective problem-solving rather than individual (and potentially selfish or solipsistic) responses.

Notes

1 See Postmes and Brunsting (2002, 300): the "Internet would appear to exert a mobilizing influence, certainly on those who are ideologically sympathetic to the causes that are widely represented online."
2 See Milota (2014) for an empirical study of online commentaries on Goodreads.
3 Soulsring games are not the only games to embrace asynchronous multiplayer, of course. *Death Stranding* (Kojima Productions 2019) is another recent game that implements a similar system. For discussion of community building and connection in *Death Stranding*, see Green (2021).
4 See, e.g., this Reddit thread: https://www.reddit.com/r/gaming/comments/j8vbj9/why_do_people_always_say_git_gud_instead_of/.
5 See, for example, FightinCowboy's beginner's guide to *ER* PvP, which goes over many of these unwritten rules: https://youtu.be/lA9uqI1KjSo.
6 For more on the GamerGate, I refer to helpful discussion by Kagen (2017) and Murray (2017, 35–42).
7 Another study by Ballard and Welch (2017), also with a focus on massively multiplayer online games and a larger sample size ($n = 151$), found that 52% of participants experienced cyberbullying.
8 See Alenda Chang's (2019, chap. 5) discussion of ecological collapse in video games.

9 See also Vella's (2015) reading of the first *Dark Souls* game (FromSoftware 2011): "for the majority of time she spends engaging with *Dark Souls*, the player will be acutely aware of the limits of her knowledge in the face of elements or behaviours in the game that the cosmos she has established cannot account for."

10 I distributed this survey on the subreddits for the three *Dark Souls* games and *Elden Ring*.

11 The whole thread can be found here: https://www.reddit.com/r/Eldenring/comments/t3xk48/what_exactly_are_those_white_ghosts_running_around/.

12 For an example of how messages can assist with puzzle-solving, see the discussion of a puzzle that requires the player to use the "Erudition" gesture in Valentine (2022).

13 https://youtu.be/keIWG6hSD7Q.

14 See this subreddit for this and a number of other examples: https://www.reddit.com/r/Eldenring/comments/t581gr/funniest_message/.

5 Levels of Interpretation in Online Discussion

In June 2022, a few months after *Elden Ring's* (*ER*'s) release, YouTube user Ratatoskr published a video titled "*Elden Ring*'s Lore Is Uninterpretable."[1] Throughout his other posts, Ratatoskr expresses deep admiration for FromSoftware's achievement, but this video starts on a more critical note, with the author observing that the game falls short of the expectations he had before release. His initial aspiration, he explains, had been to become an avid lore commentator—where lore refers, as discussed previously, to the sum total of the game's (back)stories. Ratatoskr adds that, unlike other YouTubers, he has always been more invested in symbolic or thematic meanings than in reconstructing the narrative particulars that make up the lore: "My real focus, my real interest, is and always has been the metaphorical meanings of the lore. I wanted to talk about the message the game is trying to convey, I wanted to talk about the theme, I wanted to figure out what the theme was and then relate it, in a stylish way, to everybody else; not just explain what happened, but explain what I think it all means." Yet the game keeps resisting his efforts to make sense of the lore on a thematic level—hence the disappointment and the titular verdict of "uninterpretability." As the video continues, however, the distinction between understanding the story of *ER* and interpreting its thematic meanings becomes increasingly blurry. Adopting what I discussed as an archaeological mode of fandom, Ratatoskr offers some speculations on the game's narratives: he pays close attention to the game world, including item descriptions, dialogue lines spoken by the characters, and physical features of their bodies or of the game environment. But this discussion, which is so meticulously detailed that Ratatoskr himself calls it "unhinged" and "crazy," results in an impasse: it is exceedingly hard, he argues, to draw conclusions about the characters' motivations or how they are related in terms of *ER*'s timeline. The layers of the game's narrative lead to a multitude of lore theories, which are developed and shared on internet platforms, but (to quote again from Ratatoskr's video) "there is nothing resembling a consensus." In this respect, Ratatoskr adds, *ER* differs from the *Dark Souls* (*DS*) series, whose fans have been able to agree on the basic coordinates of the narrative.

DOI: 10.4324/9781032684024-6

The intelligibility of the games' stories in *DS* has real consequences for interpretation, Ratatoskr continues. The consensus surrounding *DS* narratives brings into focus the thematic forces that shape the *DS* universe: "I believe that the high concepts [of the *DS* series], like fire and dark, are metaphorical, and that they mean something in real life; … the lore itself is a mechanism by which the overarching theme is revealed." By contrast, identifying an overarching theme is impossible in *ER*: "I don't understand what *Elden Ring* is trying to tell me." The result is that Ratatoskr "gives up." However, this intellectual gesture doesn't detract from his appreciation of the game, as he points out in the video's ending.

Ratatoskr's commentary illustrates the challenges that surround the interpretation of Soulsring games. On the level of both gameplay and narrative, the difficulty and obscurity of these games ask us to confront complex questions about digital artifacts as meaning making systems. One can't say that Ratatoskr's solution to these problems is fully satisfactory: the distinction he is drawing between *ER* and *DS* can be questioned, and it is far from clear why the obscurity of *ER*'s plot (which is one level of interpretation) would necessarily impact the interpreter's ability to work out its thematic meanings (which are located on a different level of interpretation). After all, literature offers numerous examples of works (Samuel Beckett's fiction comes to mind) that lack narrative coherence but have been relentlessly mined for thematic meanings by literary scholars. Ratatoskr thus seems to be working with a flawed, or at least reductive, understanding of interpretation. Nevertheless, it is remarkable that he was able to articulate this kind of interpretive difficulty on YouTube, receiving over 100,000 views and 1,500 comments (as of May 2023): this response shows how close the FromSoftware community comes to thorny scholarly questions on the scope and limits of interpretation. In fact, the main argument of this chapter is that Soulsring games raise interpretive challenges that call for a sophisticated and self-aware approach, particularly in the context of online fan discussions. The interactions one finds on platforms such as YouTube form an integral part of the players' interpretive investment in the games, and they can be surprisingly nuanced. Of course, any form of interpretation is grounded in "interpretive communities," to use Stanley Fish's (1980) terminology: meaning is always negotiated in interaction with shared cultural assumptions, institutional practices (e.g., literary criticism in Western academia), and intersubjective contexts (for instance, a book club or classroom). This is true of objects of interpretation in general, and video games are no exception. Increasingly, however, the internet creates new opportunities for the interpretation of a wide range of cultural texts, as demonstrated by the growing popularity of platforms such as BookTube and BookTok, two reading communities on YouTube and TikTok (see, e.g., Birke 2021).

In the case of games, too, and especially games with communities as large and dedicated as Soulsring, meaning making takes place intersubjectively through a variety of internet channels, from subreddits to YouTube videos such as Ratatoskr's. The close integration of Soulsring gameplay and community building, as discussed in the previous chapter, contributes to these sharing practices. My argument here unfolds in a series of steps. I first discuss how the interpretive efforts of commentators such as Ratatoskr are related to both players' in-game experiences and professional game scholarship. To do so, I introduce the concept of "interpretation spectrum" and I argue that online commentaries such as Ratatoskr's fall halfway between the interpretation built into game experiences and the elaborate readings one finds in game criticism. I also foreground what Liesbeth Korthals Altes (2014) calls the "metahermeneutic" dimension of such commentaries—that is, their tendency toward explicit reflection on their own interpretive practices and assumptions.

In a second step, I outline recent debates on interpretation in game studies to highlight the unique features of game hermeneutics, including its blend of narrative, thematic significance, and meanings emerging from gameplay. Finally, I develop two case studies on Soulsring interpretation as an intersubjective practice. The first consists of an analysis of the comments posted in response to Ratatoskr's video on the supposed "uninterpretability" of *ER*. The second focuses on a recurrent theme in commentaries on *DS* games, which signals the collective sharing of a more personal form of interpretation: *DS* players articulating, on both YouTube and Reddit, how gameplay helped them cope with depression. Throughout this chapter I focus on the complexity of the interpretive engagements elicited by Soulsring gameplay: in many players' responses, the hermeneutic articulation of meaning is traversed and complicated by either metahermeneutic reflection or by reflection on how the player's own self was transformed by game experiences. Extending this book's central argument, my account thus shows that the narrative and thematic complexity of Soulsring games offers an opportunity for equally complex interpretive practices, which can be seen at work on numerous internet platforms.

The Interpretation Spectrum

The word interpretation has a remarkably large scope. In the most general sense of the word, any perceptual or emotional act requires interpretation: at a basic level, experience involves making sense of the world in light of established values or concepts. If I turn a corner and notice a snake hissing on the sidewalk, my surprise and fear are an interpretation of this unexpected situation; they are an instinctual, gut response suggesting that the value of self-preservation might be at stake (the snake as a potential threat). This view of interpretation is consistent with the enactivist account of cognition I adopted and developed in previous works, influenced by Francisco Varela, Evan Thompson, and Eleanor Rosch's seminal *The Embodied Mind* (1991) and by theorists of emotion such as Giovanna Colombetti (2013). From this enactivist perspective, any act of perception or emotional response is interpretive in nature, even if it doesn't require inferential or conceptual thinking. However, when the word interpretation is used in the context of literary or game studies, it tends to refer to a much more specialized form of meaning making. In the narrowest sense, an interpretation is a verbal text offering a perspective on the meanings of a semiotic object; interpretations circulate within practices such as criticism or scholarship and are subject to certain criteria: they must illuminate the cultural artifact they engage with, they must address the interests of an interpretive community, and they must be rhetorically well constructed and based on textual particulars.[2]

Halfway between the general and the specialized sense of the word interpretation, there is a third way in which we can use the term: we can say that any form of engagement with a cultural work such as a novel or a video game involves interpretation, even if it doesn't result in overt statements about the work's meanings. Put more simply, interpretation is not necessarily a written text subject to certain conventions; it is a meaning making activity that underlies our experience of a work, including our emotional responses, immersion, character engagement, and so on. This is, after all, consistent with the fact that there is meaning generation at work when we parse the verbal or audiovisual language of a novel, play, or video game. The real-time and low-level interpretation that unfolds as we engage with an artifact also covers a broad spectrum. In literary theory, Peter Lamarque (2008, 141–51) has drawn a distinction between explication, elucidation, and interpretation proper. The first concerns linguistic meaning (e.g., what did Shakespeare mean by "mortal coil"?), while the second has to do with working out what happens in a story (for instance, keeping track of the plot of *Hamlet* as we read the play or watch a performance). Interpretation proper involves articulating the thematic "aboutness" of a text: the problem or concern it engages with or negotiates (for instance, one could interpret *Hamlet* as capturing the tensions and contradictions of early modern subjectivity). All of these forms of interpretation are at work in games, but we should add a form of real-time interpretation that is unique to gameplay since it focuses on the significance of game mechanics and rules. For example, playing a video game adaptation of *Hamlet* (such as *Elsinore* [Golden Glitch 2019]) requires understanding the mechanics that allow players to pursue the game's objectives and advance the narrative. This is also an act of interpretation that builds on language comprehension but cannot be reduced to it.

To summarize, the word interpretation falls on a spectrum (see figure 5.1) that goes from (1) any form of meaning making while engaging with the world to (2) making sense of semiotic artifacts as we engage with them and (3) producing verbal commentary on the same artifacts as we participate in structured activities such as cultural criticism or scholarship.[3] Interpretation 2 can be further subdivided into a number of levels, depending on whether it homes

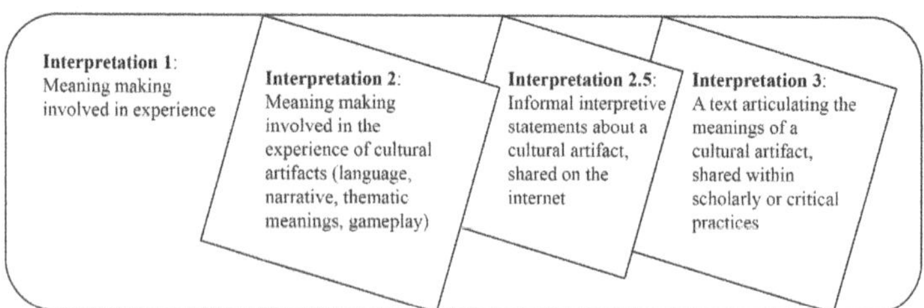

Figure 5.1 A visual representation of the interpretation spectrum (author's creation).

in on verbal language, narrative, gameplay, or thematic significance. Even more importantly perhaps, interpretation 2 is experiential and affective, since meaning making (on all of the aforementioned levels) is driven by emotional responses and interests. There has been a tendency in literary theory to draw a sharp distinction between interpretations 2 and 3, based on the assumption of a fundamental difference between the affective meanings involved in the experience of literature and the more conceptual meanings that are part and parcel of scholarship. Hans Ulrich Gumbrecht's (2004) opposition of embodied presence and meaning works in this way, for example, and (well before Gumbrecht) Susan Sontag's (2001) essay "Against Interpretation" also presented experience and literary-critical interpretation as incompatible stances. The differences between the spontaneous meaning making of experience and critical or scholarly commentary are real, but it is important to keep in mind that both activities are invested in meaning generation, and also that they are both variously bound up with intersubjective practices.

Regardless of its sophistication, interpretation in both senses 2 and 3 involves working out the relevance of a cultural artifact by mapping it onto a background of personal or cultural concerns. For instance, one could say that the extreme difficulty of Soulsring games, combined with the landscape of devastation in which they routinely immerse the player, captures the existential dread of living in times of ecological crisis. Ecological concerns are thus the background for my reading of the games—a figure-ground structure reminiscent of Gestalt psychology.[4] This interpretation could be a mere thought I have while I play the games, and perhaps not so much an articulate thought as an emotional experience vaguely connected to environmental themes—interpretation in my sense 2. Or it could be the basis for a scholarly article on the ecocritical significance of Soulsring games (interpretation in my sense 3). These are profoundly different interpretive acts, at least in terms of their outcome, but they are grounded in the same gesture of projecting a certain aspect of experience onto a background of significance that is, in some way, socially shared.

What if I do what Ratatoskr and many other Soulsring fans do, though, and post an online video or comment explicating the ecological resonance of the games? My statement would fall somewhere between interpretations 2 and 3: it would be grounded in first-hand experience of the game but articulated verbally for the benefit of the fan community, in a less formalized context than game criticism. This is what I call "interpretation 2.5" (see again figure 5.1), a name that suggests the in-betweenness of this type of response but also the difficulty of drawing sharp distinctions within the interpretation spectrum. As I will show in the next pages, fan practices of this kind may be less structured than cultural criticism, but they are capable of significant sophistication, not only through the close attention they devote to game worlds (the archaeological mindset I discussed previously) but also because they display self-reflectiveness on multiple levels. Some of the interpretations 2.5 I consider engage in what Liesbeth Korthals Altes (2014) has termed a "metahermeneutic" approach: they reflect on the assumptions that underlie interpretive practices. For instance, in response to Ratatoskr's judgment of unfathomability for *ER*, commentators could trace a distinction between the kind of "closed" meaning that Ratatoskr is looking for in the game (and failing to find) and a more open-ended understanding of the game's significance. Such statements combine a hermeneutic stance (attempting to make sense of the game) and metahermeneutic thinking on one's own interpretive biases and how they both differ from and relate to the meanings constructed by other players. This collective dimension is highlighted by Korthals Altes's discussion of metahermeneutic thinking: "metahermeneutic reflection emphasizes that procedures for reasoning and criteria of rigor need to be defined intersubjectively" (2014, 48).

In other instances, as we will see, interpretation 2.5 is accompanied by self-reflection instead of metareflection in Korthals Altes's sense. Simply put, commentators draw on game interpretation to deepen understanding of their own self and personal experiences, for example (in my case study), by foregrounding the transformative potential of Soulsring gameplay during a mental health crisis. Thus, the sophistication of interpretation 2.5 derives from its blend of hermeneutic and reflective tendencies. That sophistication is often supported by intersubjective contexts (e.g., Reddit or YouTube) in which a commentator participates in dialogue with other players, by responding to their interpretations or by inviting (dis)agreement.

Interpretation 2.5 is not exclusive to *ER* or FromSoftware games, of course. But the complexity of these games serves as a catalyst for this type of (meta)hermeneutic response, inspiring players to bring to bear a wide range of preoccupations and interests in their game experiences and sharing them online. My goal here is to scrutinize how this interpretive process unfolds and how it is shaped by the affordances of digital media platforms. Of course, to fully understand how this type of interpretation works, we need to consider the specificities of game hermeneutics.

Approaches to Game Hermeneutics

Jonne Arjoranta asks: "how do games differ as objects of interpretation from other hermeneutic objects? First, they are procedural systems. Second, they are interactive. Third, they are temporally complex" (2011, 9). I have already discussed at length the temporally complex layering of Soulsring games. As Arjoranta points out, temporal complexity is further complicated by the interactivity of game systems—that is, by the fact that they require input from the player. Arjoranta also builds on Bogost's concept of procedurality: video games are procedural in that their responses to the player's input aren't fixed but derive, in real time, from a set of constraints and rules. Both interactivity and procedurality are integral parts of processes of meaning generation in games. Take, for instance, the infamous difficulty of Soulsring combat: this difficulty is "ergodic" rather than merely interpretive, to lift Espen Aarseth's (1997) distinction, since "nontrivial" effort (in the forms of skills and knowledge of enemy positioning and capabilities) is required to progress through the games. Further, the difficulty is procedural in that it arises from interactions among the games' rules: for instance, the enemies' number, large health pool, considerable damage output, the short time span of damage negation offered by the dodge mechanic, and so on. Interactivity and procedurality set video games apart from cultural objects such as novels and films, but that doesn't mean that these features of video game systems do not feed into interpretation: on the contrary, any respectable interpretation of a video game must take into account how its procedural nature and its structural openness to the player's input shape meaning generation.

Aarseth himself, writing about game interpretation in an article with Sebastian Möring, argues that "the postulated hermeneutics of computer games can … be understood as a hermeneutics of the interplay between mechanics and semiotics" (Aarseth and Möring 2020, 2). This suggests that game interpretation needs to consider both the representational (semiotic) level of games, including the narratives they tell, and the meanings created by the (interactive, procedural) mechanics of gameplay. Michał Kłosiński (2022) offers a useful overview of methodological steps in video game interpretation: in line with Aarseth and Möring's work, his account starts with the game itself—particularly engagement with gameplay mechanics as well as narrative content. Conveniently for us, Kłosiński uses *ER* as his main example, illustrating how his ten steps disclose different—and increasingly complex—aspects of the FromSoftware title. These steps are as follows: (1) gameplay experience, with the meaning making that underlies it (interpretation 2 in my terminology); (2) distancing oneself from direct experience, a stance that "enables the analyst to relate their own perspective toward what others have written or said about the game"; (3) problematizing one's assumptions about the game (which may be derived from previous gaming experiences, the media, or other players' commentary); (4) coming up with a short summary of the game; (5)

identifying the interpretive problems that the game raises; (6) reconstructing the way in which the game evokes meaning, for instance through symbolism; (7) challenging the game's own meaning making strategies by reading against the grain of the developers' intentions (a phase that Kłosiński calls "suspicion"); (8) invoking a certain theoretical framework or question ("theoretical coupling"); (9) articulating the game's existential or personal appeal ("What does the game mean to me as addressed to me?"); and, lastly, (10) testing one's hypotheses "by producing them for a specialized community."

The kind of back-and-forth Kłosiński has in mind also combines a hermeneutic agenda with the potential for metahermeneutic reflection, to use again Korthals Altes's terminology, for example, when certain assumptions are problematized or when taking a step back from gameplay allows the commentator to compare notes with other interpreters. Kłosiński makes clear that not all of the steps he discusses are mandatory, and that they are not meant to be followed in sequence; however, his reference to "theoretical coupling" and a "specialized community" suggests that his primary way of thinking about interpretation is close to my interpretation 3—that is, interpretation as practiced by game scholars through explicit verbal commentary. Nevertheless, virtually all aspects of his model apply to interpretation 2.5 as well, with the caveat that many of the conceptual operations game critics consciously go through will take place implicitly as players attempt to make sense of a game. Moreover, in interpretation 2.5 Kłosiński's "theoretical framework" (step 8) is likely to take a back seat to existential or personal relevance (step 9), even though of course there can be no personal relevance without a pool of interests (a "framework" in an extended sense) that are at least potentially shared with others. In fact, one way in which Kłosiński's account of game hermeneutics could be augmented is by devoting more attention to the intersubjective nature of meaning making. That is why the internet interpretations and discussions of Soulsring games I examine in the following pages are so significant: they demonstrate different pathways for the articulation of relevance, but they also show how these meanings are shaped within participatory practices that—much like literary or game criticism—value articulateness of expression and the ability to enter a reflective dialogue with others. The unique complexity of FromSoftware games is thus reflected in the interpretive efforts that surround them.

Negotiating Uninterpretability

Let us revisit Ratatoskr's video in light of the concepts introduced in the previous pages. As I mentioned, Ratatoskr addresses two dimensions of *ER* lore, which roughly correspond to Lamarque's (2008) "elucidation" and "interpretation proper." Elucidation involves reconstructing a narrative sequence—that is, what happened to whom, where, and on what occasion. For Ratatoskr, the sparseness of narrative clues provided by *ER* makes complete elucidation impossible: considered as a whole, the game's lore resists narrative meaning making. That conclusion is in line with what I said in chapters 1 and 2 about the multiple complications introduced by strategies such as nonlinear or environmental storytelling. However, Ratatoskr's standards for elucidation appear to be unreasonably high: *ER* does contain multiple narrative strands that are perfectly intelligible, but it refuses to spell out the connections between those strands in an unambiguous fashion. Ratatoskr is making claims about Lamarque's interpretation proper, too, since he laments the absence of a single "overarching theme" pursued by the lore. Indeed, narrative and thematic dimensions appear to be closely bound up in the discussion: it is because there is no consensus on the lore's narrative that the game becomes uninterpretable in thematic terms, too, and this in contradistinction to *DS*, in which (again, according to Ratatoskr) narrative and thematic relevance remain more in focus.

Many players disagree with Ratatoskr's judgment of uninterpretability, even as they mostly agree with him about the difficulty of articulating the game's significance both narratively and thematically. This is what emerges from my analysis of the over 1,500 comments posted on YouTube in response to the video. Through these responses to Ratatoskr (and to other players' comments), YouTube users attempt to negotiate intersubjectively the interpretive difficulties posed by *ER*. Not only do the commentators discuss what struck them as the game's main themes, but they connect those themes to personal and existential concerns and also to metahermeneutic reflection on the standards and assumptions that underlie interpretation. In this way, YouTube users perform many of the operations discussed by Kłosiński in relation to professional game criticism.

Obviously, going by the number of likes and replies, not all comments enjoy the same degree of popularity and attention. However, even restricting the analysis to the ten comments that received more than 100 likes reveals a surprising diversity in players' responses to the game.[5] I will tease out some of the motifs that recur throughout these responses, focusing on these ten most popular comments but referring to some of the other comments as well to support the analysis. I will address these motifs in order of increasing sophistication, defining sophistication (an admittedly partial definition) as the commentator's ability to shift between hermeneutic discussion of the game and metahermeneutic reflection in Korthals Altes's sense.

We start from comments that contradict Ratatoskr's hesitation (and the uninterpretability verdict that results from it) by simply stating what the commentator thought was the game's main theme. This strategy tends to downplay the game's interpretive ambiguity, but it can still result in nuanced and stimulating readings; Fabrimuch, for instance, remarks: "I like to think of *Elden Ring* as FromSoft's chance to explore the themes they couldn't with the static world of *Dark Souls*: an examination of what meaningful change looks like, on large scale and personal as well, while *Dark Souls* was an exploration of what an extreme inability to change looked like." This interpretation is inspired by the *ER-DS* comparison contained in Ratatoskr's video, but it takes that comparison in a straightforwardly hermeneutic direction instead of engaging in metahermeneutic reflection: the difference between the two games can be expressed as an opposition between the stagnation of the *DS* universe and the radical changes that are sweeping through the world of *ER*. Other commentators point to themes such as "becoming" (FRANKIEonWCin240p), "ambition" (blackbomb), "the struggle between letting go and holding on" (VonSchnitzel), and so on. These responses show that, *pace* Ratatoskr, stating the thematic aboutness of *ER* is anything but impossible, even if this relatively straightforward interpretive strategy does reduce considerably the game's complexity.

A second strategy involves a shift from thematic interpretation to elucidation, corroborating Ratatoskr's point about the impossibility of reaching a consensus about the game's baseline narrative. In a response with over 900 likes, GILGAMESH states that "one of the major difficulties in interpreting the lore comes from the lack of any real timeline; it's why so much of the story feels all over the place." In replies to GILGAMESH, a number of commentators echo their statement. The temporal stratification I discussed in chapter 1 is said to contribute to the unintelligibility of the lore: "There's a complete lack of any sense of time at all. It's like some things feel like they happened a couple years ago and then other times it's like a thousand years which throws the lore all over the place" (NezumiXP). Other commentators, both within this thread and in response to the video directly, explain that future expansions of the game (downloadable content or DLC, as they are known in gaming terminology) can be expected to shed light on the plot's mysteries: "The DLC being the key to understanding FromSoft games is something that has pretty consistently been proven true" (cvrc11). This is related to what Yacobi (1981), as discussed in chapter 2, labels a "genetic" approach to textual ambiguities: instead of finding answers in the game itself, the interpreter appeals to the creators for more clarity (here in the form of future iterations of the game). But, again, these responses are fully invested in the hermeneutic possibility of "fixing" the game's narrative meaning.

Other interpreters share this confidence in the fact that the lore will become more interpretable in the future; however, instead of pinning their hopes on a DLC, they show trust and appreciation for the workings of the community itself, or rather of one of its subgroups. Ratatoskr is singled out as a commentator who is not afraid to express frustration and hesitations related to the game's lore, as the video itself suggests. John C (R A), for instance, comments: "People, like Ratatoskr and Crunchy OTOH, have taken a more deliberate, meditative approach to patiently working through the lore so as to avoid unnecessary confusion that could get the conversation around lore twisted in a tangled mess of knots." The admission of difficulty contained in the video is thus seen as an indication of Ratatoskr's serious and deliberate approach to lore: even if this engagement results (for now) in an unfavorable verdict, it is a more honest stance than the one adopted by YouTubers who attempt to impose coherence at all costs and end up with "a tangled mess of knots." John C (R A)'s comment on divisions internal to the lore community is thus based on metahermeneutic awareness of a conflict in standards of interpretation: the rush to produce meaning versus the more "meditative" pace of someone like Ratatoskr.

With what I call the openness motif metahermeneutic concerns also come to the fore. Numerous users allude to the scale of this FromSoftware game, which is significantly vaster than the *DS* series. In some of these responses, the open-world design is linked to the semantic openness of the game, and this is where hermeneutic engagement starts bordering on the *meta*hermeneutic. A commentator named Michael Blandino puts it as follows: "I personally feel that wandering through the Lands Between is the closest thing to wandering Mount Olympus, encountering all of the contradictory myths that have cropped up over time. Not by From's design, just that the contradiction and uncertainty is really interesting to me." A parallel with ancient Greek myth ("Mount Olympus") allows this user to appreciate the way in which the game's open world mirrors the "uncertainty" of the meanings it generates, and that includes meanings that haven't been baked into the game by the developers ("not by From's design"). Deliberately or not, these interpreters come close to Umberto Eco's (1989) influential understanding of the "open work" as an experimental text that is co-constructed by the audience. User Dан articulates this point in a more explicitly metahermeneutic fashion, in a direct response to Ratatoskr's judgment of uninterpretability: "How is the [audience] intended to receive this, you might ask? Mostly in the sense that it's a piece of art that might not fully have a meaning that can be translated directly to you, but left open for you to find your own meaning in it." Instead of resisting interpretation, *ER* enables a plurality of readings, which can prove frustrating to some players (including Ratatoskr) but is ultimately a sign of FromSoftware's artistic achievement. Instead of attempting to identify a stable meaning, interpreters start reflecting on their own practices and assumptions when confronted with a complex work.

The same combination of hermeneutic and metahermeneutic engagement is sometimes employed to establish existential relevance, to use a category from Kłosiński's game hermeneutics. At first glance, the following response (by a user named Matthew Ball) might seem to fall into my first category, that of players seeking to define the meaning of the game; but in fact, this is a much more sophisticated interpretation that *builds on* the kind of difficulty voiced by Ratatoskr and channels it toward existential significance: "I think the absurdity of being thrown into a world that you don't fully—and cannot ever fully—understand, struggling for survival, where everything is so vast and overwhelming, and yet you are still ultimately responsible for its future is the main thematic takeaway I have from the game." The game's uninterpretability is not perceived as an aesthetic flaw but rather as part of its *appeal*, since it gives rise to the unique challenge of having to determine the fate of a world we do not, and cannot, understand fully. Another user outlines a similar view: "I think Miyazaki captures real life perfectly. We live in a world of mystery, no matter how much we excavate, we will never understand the full story" (Beard is love Beard is life). Max Genecov elaborates: "in the case of *Elden Ring* especially, that experience is one of 'thrownness.' You are in a world that, realistically, refuses to explain itself to you." These responses thus deftly combine a hermeneutic and a metahermeneutic stance, the effort to work out the meaning of the game, and awareness of how it consistently thwarts our efforts.

It is not a coincidence that these (meta)hermeneutic interpretations emerge as a response to Ratatoskr's video: the context of YouTube discussion enables the fan community to debate the meanings of *ER*, exposing disagreements but also creating interpretive opportunities that would not have been available to the players based on gameplay experience alone. In short, this kind of interpretation 2.5 is a testament to the game's inherent complexity, but it also suggests that the internet discussion of FromSoftware games (and, of course, many other video games) can result in responses that, while not framed in the language of scholarship per se, come close to its complexity.

Depression and Gameplay: Transformative *Souls*

After this broad overview of interpretive strategies brought to bear on *ER*, this final section zooms in on one particular approach to the interpretation of FromSoftware games that has wide circulation on the internet: on platforms such as YouTube and Reddit, numerous players suggest that *DS* games helped them cope with depression. I will not pursue the psychological side of this claim, which I have no means of evaluating. Rather, I will foreground the rhetorical and interpretive work performed by players linking *DS* gameplay and depression: saying that *DS* games proved beneficial during a period of mental distress represents a way of negotiating the significance of these games in personal terms—that is, of interpreting the games in sense 2 and of sharing these interpretations intersubjectively through video essays or informal internet commentary (interpretation 2.5). This tendency reflects one of Kłosiński's (2022) methodological steps, namely, the articulation of a game's personal or existential relevance: in Kłosiński's words, "[existential] inquiry … focuses on the transformative functions of digital games, the power that play—as a cultural practice—holds over the individual."

As I explained above, interpretation involves projecting a certain cultural artifact onto a background of interests and concerns. In some instances (and certainly when the gameplay-depression link is invoked), the chosen background for interpretation is the interpreter's own self, which is illuminated by interaction with a cultural text. Potentially, this is also a "transformative" process, as Kłosiński acknowledges and as scholars in empirical literary studies are beginning to investigate experimentally. Olivia Fialho, for example, has developed an empirical model of "transformative reading" that aims to describe how "literature *defamiliarizes perceptions* and *modifies personal meanings*" (2019, 9). Fialho's work builds on Don Kuiken, David Miall, and Shelley Sikora's (2004) study of self-implication and self-modification in reading, which shows how literary reading can both evoke aspects of readers' sense of self and create opportunities for its transformation. For Kuiken, Miall, and Sikora, these transformations are always bound up with an affective response to literature: by eliciting "self-modifying feelings," literature (in their study, Romantic poetry) may expand readers' sense of self, clarify episodes from their past, or help them crystallize their fears and hopes for the future.

Kuiken, Miall, and Sikora also suggest that self-modifying feelings are especially likely to emerge during periods of personal crisis; their main example is depression associated with bereavement. As they show, reading poetry in the immediate aftermath of loss does not typically result in self-modification, whereas transformative reading is frequently reported after a temporal interval: "such depth in reading [leading to self-transformation] is *more* likely to occur among people who remain depressed about a temporally *remote* significant loss, an unresolved loss that nonetheless has become, with the passage of time, more accessible and acceptable" (2004, 196). There are obvious differences between Kuiken, Miall, and Sikora's empirical setup and my more informal study of internet commentaries, but there is also considerable conceptual common ground. Kuiken, Miall, and Sikora describe the affective dynamics of transformative reading during a protracted personal crisis, a model that opens up a way of thinking about how gameplay may allow *DS* players to overcome or manage depression: engagement with a cultural artifact triggers a reconsideration of personal experience that is transformative and interpretive at the same time. Like the interpretations I examined in the previous section, this dynamic can result in fairly complex readings, which blend hermeneutic engagement and reflection. However, instead of reflection on hermeneutic modes and practices, which was present in several responses to Ratatoskr's video, the link between *DS* experience and depression foregrounds *self*-reflection. Metahermeneutic engagement and self-modifying feelings share an intersubjective dynamic: in both cases, the FromSoftware internet community provides a context for sharing these interpretations, enabling the negotiation of personal meanings in dialogue with similarly transformative responses.

A simple YouTube search for "*Dark Souls* and depression" reveals a handful of videos discussing the *DS* series' link to mental health issues. One of the most articulate of these videos was posted by a YouTuber named Hamish Black on the "Writing on Games" channel.[6] Black starts by surveying claims on the extreme difficulty of *DS* games, but then goes on to suggest that—for all their bleakness and frustrations—the series can be read as an "uncompromising … celebration of life." This seemingly paradoxical reading, he adds, "comes from a very personal place"—namely, a period of severe depression and anxiety that culminated in multiple suicide attempts. The video takes its cue from the insight that the YouTuber's "experiences with suicidal depression and [his] experiences with *Dark Souls* resonate with each other in some pretty odd ways." For Black, this resonance has two foci: the difficulty of *DS* gameplay, which mirrors the daily struggle of mental illness; and the way in which *DS* games withhold agency from the player by displaying the player-character's insignificance vis-à-vis the history of the *DS* universe or also by denying them the linear teleology of a quest narrative. As Black puts it (echoing some of my claims about nonlinear storytelling in chapter 1), "it's easy for the goal to become obfuscated to the player—for them to forget what the larger narrative even is …. The player's goals, as a result, become, one, making the experience in this cold, indifferent world as bearable as it possibly can be—because there is joy to behold in this world if you can get past that; and, two, reclaim as much agency within this world as you possibly can." The player is thus forced to work on what Black calls the "small things"—particularly mastering the deep mechanics of combat, but also taking in the intricate detail and impressive vistas of the games' locations. Unlike most other games, the player's progress is slow, because the game doesn't hold their hand; yet the more players have to train themselves to defeat a certain boss or clear an area, the more emotional rewards the game yields on account of its difficulty. For Black, these gradual gameplay improvements served as a blueprint for implementing real-life changes that, while seemingly mundane, proved instrumental in managing his depression.

It is important to note that Black's claim about *DS* experience and mental illness is grounded in a certain interpretation of the games, an interpretation that elegantly brings together gameplay and narrative design: the challenges posed by *DS* games encapsulate an existential insight that *could* fold into nihilism but is actually redeemed by the positive emotional values of the combat as well as of the complex narrative and spatial design. It is perhaps not unwarranted to invoke the Aristotelian notion of catharsis for this transformation of feelings—from the negative emotions aroused by the bleakness of the game world to empowerment through growing familiarity with game systems.[7] Black's interpretation thus builds on his emotional engagement with the games (interpretation in sense 2) but also articulates how these emotions led to a transformative experience which had a significant impact on his daily life, including his depression. Moreover, he adds that the games' multiplayer community helped him feel connected at a time of severe isolation—a sense of connectedness that he is, arguably, performing by posting this video to a YouTube channel.

The responses to the video are overwhelmingly sympathetic and add a variety of perspectives on the gameplay-depression link. Many players express admiration for Black's decision to publish a video that openly discusses sensitive experiences of depression and self-harm. Some commentators note that Black's comments (on the level of interpretation 2.5) present a lucid articulation of their own experience of the game (interpretation 2): "I've been depressed for more than 10 years now and we have the same experiences from playing *Dark Souls*. You just eloquently placed it into awesome words!" (Dango Man). Another commentator (friendlySkeletor) links a history of depression to a preference for helping players who are struggling with *DS* bosses: the suggestion is that selfless, collaborative play has its own emotional rewards, and that they may also contribute to alleviating depressive tendencies. Equally intriguing are responses that, while echoing Black's sentiment, add a twist to his reading of *DS*: V T, for example, states (with more than 900 likes) that "*Dark Souls* made me understand Buddhism. Seriously. I was a Buddhist all my life, but I never really understand it. Then playing *Dark Souls* and it dawns on me … The world is full of pain and suffering, so the only way to move forward is to relax and drink in the atmosphere. Just enjoy the moment to moment wonder and take the failure as it is." This reading revisits the discussion of "small things" in Black's video but conjugates it in the language of Buddhist thinking. The self-modifying dynamic is clear-cut here: the experience of gameplay, supported by a particular (if, until this moment, implicit) interpretation of the game, illuminates an aspect of the player's self ("it dawns on me"). While this transformative experience took place before watching Black's video, the YouTuber's open discussion of mental health issues created a context in which this player (and many others) could reflect on their own experiences. To reiterate this chapter's throughline, the Soulsring internet community makes it possible for players to share *and* simultaneously clarify the personal or cultural significance of the games through collective meaning making.

Reddit discussions present a strikingly similar picture. A post upvoted by more than a 1,000 users discusses *DS* as "one of the most therapeutic games that I've ever played."[8] The author of the initial post, grandmasterpmd, closes with the words "Don't you dare go hollow," which are lifted from dialogue with an NPC in *DS1*, the aspiring pyromancer Laurentius. This line comes up repeatedly in discussions of depression and *DS*, almost as a mantra encapsulating the personal significance of gameplay. As one of the Reddit users (Ptidus) explains in response to grandmasterpmd, the hollowing mechanic (see chapter 3) is "a great metaphor for depression": "Don't you dare go hollow" outlines a parallel between persevering with *DS* gameplay despite its significant difficulties and not giving in to the spiral of depression. The same player refers to the character who speaks this line, Laurentius, and comments on the fact that he goes hollow himself after trying, and failing, to imitate the player-character's persistence. This ironic conclusion points to the player's unwitting implication in morally undesirable outcomes, an aspect of the complexity of Soulsring games that I will take up in the next chapter. Notable here is how, in the dynamic of this subreddit, an initial statement on the transformative value of *DS* gameplay leads to more collective interpretation, in the form of a re-examination of the games' narrative. Reddit user thegreenhat thanks Ptidus for the new insight into Laurentius they have offered through their "Don't you dare go hollow" commentary: "Over 4 years later and I'm still discovering new layers to this game. Never thought of his [Laurentius's] story that way before but that's so accurate." Instead of only dealing with generalities, this Reddit thread shows how closely commentators can tie the articulation of personal relevance to hermeneutic investment in individual aspects of gameplay (such as a single character or storyline). This link suggests that the self-reported effects of gameplay are always based on a particular interpretation of the games' narrative and thematic significance; moreover, this significance is enhanced and deepened when interpretation becomes an act of collective meaning making through the mediation of the internet.

***

Not only are Soulsring games uniquely complex from a conceptual and narrative perspective, as this book has argued extensively, but their interpretive puzzles favor equally nuanced and elaborate readings. YouTube user Ratatoskr captures this difficulty by discussing the "uninterpretability" of *ER* lore, which both resists narrative reconstruction and disrupts the players' quest for thematic or symbolic significance. However, rather than foreclosing interpretation, the games' ambiguity and opacity serve as a catalyst for a wide range of readings, as the responses to Ratatoskr's video suggest. This chapter has positioned such responses vis-à-vis current debates on interpretation in both literary theory and game studies. Literary theorists highlight the breadth of the net cast by the word interpretation, which can be used loosely for any form of meaning making, including the prereflective meanings that underlie experience in general (the level of what I called interpretation 1) and the experience of cultural artifacts in particular (interpretation 2). Interpretation is also used as shorthand for the explicit verbal commentaries found in cultural criticism, including literary and game studies (interpretation 3). Internet discussions of games, such as *DS* and *ER,* occupy a significant position on this "interpretation spectrum": they are based on the low-level interpretation of experience (interpretation 2) but through their verbal and intersubjective form they approximate the sophistication of critical readings (interpretation 3). For that reason, I used the term interpretation 2.5 to refer to the interpretive responses that circulate in internet-based practices.

In my analysis of online debates on Soulsring games, the sophistication of interpretation 2.5 becomes particularly salient in statements that combine two stances: a properly hermeneutic stance, which is invested in the production of narrative or thematic meanings, and a reflective stance, which the chapter's case studies conjugate in two different ways. In the discussion generated by Ratatoskr's video, many users underscore the assumptions and standards involved in interpretation itself, particularly the idea (implicit in Ratatoskr's commentary) that interpretation requires consensus on the baseline narrative of a game instead of acceptance of the plurality or openness of the game's meanings. These responses, which represent a substantial portion of the sample, juggle hermeneutic and metahermeneutic interests. My second case study dealt with readings from the *DS* series that draw a link between the difficulty of gameplay and the player's ability to overcome or manage depression. Without evaluating the medical validity of this claim, I foregrounded the rhetorical and interpretive operation performed by players who, on YouTube and Reddit, articulate the games' therapeutic value. I suggested that this negotiation of the games' relevance bears a close resemblance to transformative reading and self-modifying feelings, concepts through which empirical literary scholars express literature's power to implicate and transform the reader's self. Similarly, discussions on depression and *DS* games reveal how the series is able to crystallize negative emotions (of difficulty, bleakness, frustration, etc.) and direct them toward an expanded sense of control and appreciation of detail. Many players ground this claim about the games' therapeutic effect in an existential interpretation that considers both *DS* mechanics and the elusive narratives that traverse the game world. Hermeneutic engagement and self-reflection thus go hand in hand.

Also significant, as I have highlighted throughout, is the fact that this interpretive complexity emerges in a dialogic context: it may build on individual experiences, but the FromSoftware community plays a pivotal role in fostering sophisticated responses to the games, through the interchanges that are made possible by platforms such as YouTube or Reddit. As I discussed in the previous chapter, FromSoftware games achieve a close integration of gameplay experience and community: this integration also creates an ideal environment for sharing interpretations whose complexity is enhanced by the possibility of intersubjective confrontation. The next chapter turns to a particular domain in which Soulsring games foster complex thinking—that of ethical reasoning.

Notes

1 https://youtu.be/dgpy_-Eeet0.
2 In Caracciolo (2016), I call these the "textual," "interest," and "rhetorical" criteria, respectively.
3 For further discussion of this "interpretation spectrum," see Caracciolo (2014).
4 See Caracciolo (2016, 188–89) for this figure-ground structure of any interpretive act.
5 These are comments posted by the following users: GILGAMESH, cvrc11, Matthew Ball, DROP TABLE FROM, C. B., Arturo Macor, Karl Klein, Connor Ryan, fabrimuch, and BSnocomply. I am not including here a pinned post by Ratatoskr himself, which also received more than 100 likes. The text was collected

from https://youtu.be/dgpy_-Eeet0 on January 30, 2023, and only lightly edited for grammar and clarity.

6 https://youtu.be/viP4psS3MUQ.

7 The concept of catharsis tends to be used in a more reductive way in game studies, particularly in the context of empirical research on the real-world effects of in-game violence (see, e.g., Ferguson et al. 2014).

8 https://www.reddit.com/r/darksouls/comments/3okk3g/dark_souls_and_depression/.

6 Soul and Swamp

Ethics of Soulsring Gameplay

Prima facie, the plot of Soulsring games involves a simple, even dichotomous moral universe. In *DS*, "linking" the First Flame to extend the current Age of Fire would seem to be a life-affirming, morally desirable gesture, whereas bringing about the beginning of the Age of Dark has the opposite connotations. The clash between the Golden Order and its detractors (including the chaos-loving followers of the Frenzied Flame) in *ER* fulfills a similar role and can also be mapped rather straightforwardly onto a moral dichotomy between good and evil. Such oppositions are anything but unusual in the fantasy genre, of course. Writing about J. R. R. Tolkien's *The Lord of the Rings*, Lionel Basney argues that "Tolkien's crucial modification of moral issues is to simplify them—to omit 'complexities, complications, subtleties' in favor of choices determined by established character, by vaguely adduced modes of causality, and by a contextual morality built into the cosmology of Middle-earth" (1980, 24).[1] The fire versus dark (or Golden Order versus chaos) dichotomy in Soulsring also aligns the cosmological setup of the games with their basic moral coordinates. However, as this chapter will discuss, this association is consistently complicated by gameplay and narrative mechanics that undermine the player's attempts to determine the ethical stakes of the game world and its characters. This does not mean that Soulsring games are completely amoral: on the contrary, they keep evoking ethical values and making players complicit in actions whose consequences they could not have fully anticipated; yet it is difficult, if not impossible, for players to resolve the meaning of good and evil in the Soulsring universe. This ambiguity, as I will argue here, is highly productive in that it stimulates the player's ethical meaning making without spoon-feeding them with moral certainties. This potential for ethical self-reflection is made evident by Reddit or YouTube arguments on the games' morality: even players who dislike FromSoftware's approach to moral decision-making engage with ethical significance in a way that is uncommon in more conventional fantasy works.[2]

Matthew Kelly has already discussed the ethics of *DS* games by underscoring their potential for "rethinking how we approach ethical responsibility amid our current technological and socio-cultural circumstances" (2016).

DOI: 10.4324/9781032684024-7

Largely, Kelly's account centers on the ethical value of community building and converges with my argument on how the difficulty of Soulsring games, along with their constrained multiplayer, creates opportunities for interpersonal connection and meaningful online discussion (see chapters 4 and 5). In this chapter, I will shift the focus to community building as a response to a particular kind of *ethical* difficulty that is staged by *DS* games and *ER*. Soulsring games undermine the player's moral calculus through the strategic uncertainty that surrounds the NPCs' quests and the games' multiple endings. To fully unpack that argument, I will proceed in four steps: I will first discuss the moral significance of fiction (including video games) as a negotiation of ethical values, and I will focus on a particular kind of negotiation that brings audiences face-to-face with forms of moral complexity and difficulty. I will then turn to the specific means through which video games as an interactive medium can negotiate moral difficulties. Third, I will illustrate all this through examples taken from Soulsring games, devoting particular attention to the NPCs' storylines and the endings. Lastly, I will explore a recurrent trope in Soulsring games—the poison swamp—as a spatial allegory that captures the games' fascination with difficulty through the integration of gameplay and moral challenges. This convergence of gameplay and ethical difficulty, I will argue in the book's coda, is the most striking manifestation of the games' literary complexity.

Negotiating Ethical Values through Fiction

A great amount of ink has been spilled on the ethics of fiction, in both the philosophy of art and literary studies. To many, talk about the "ethics of fiction" suggests that fictional texts may be used to train or deepen moral reasoning—that is, the thinking we do to arrive at conclusions about what is right or wrong in moral terms. Typically, that process involves judging a certain situation (real or fictional) in light of the ethical values we hold. (A rule-of-thumb distinction is that morality applies to the domain of concrete human action and behavior, whereas ethics has to do with the abstract principles that guide human conduct, or the philosophical discussion thereof; in practice, though, it is sometimes difficult to differentiate between morality and ethics, which is why I will use the two terms interchangeably in what follows.[3])

One of the most influential positions in the field of literary ethics was articulated by Wayne Booth (1988), for whom readers of fiction engage in a sustained dialogue with the author's own ethical evaluations. Booth uses the metaphor of friendship to discuss the way in which literary works encourage a sharing of values from authors to readers—with the readers, of course, being free to reject those values or only adopt them temporarily, for the duration of their engagement with the text. Using an Aristotelian term, Booth refers to those values collectively as the author's "ethos." Also working within a neo-Aristotelian framework, Martha Nussbaum (e.g., 2010) takes these ideas further, suggesting that literature is central to the cultivation of the values that underlie modern liberal democracies.

An essential point throughout these discussions is that whatever moral influence fiction may have should *not* be understood as a simple act of imparting a certain value (or set of values) to the audience members.[4] At its best, fiction isn't a mere delivery mechanism for moral ideals but rather a "moral laboratory"—to use Frank Hakemulder's (2000) phrase—that enables audiences to clarify, reflect on, and possibly question their own ethical values through confrontation with fictional characters and events. Even when fiction does try to convey a moral system to its audiences, they are likely to reframe or rework the proffered moral values in light of their own experiences and interpretations. This is the kind of nonlinear relationship Booth has in mind when he talks about books as friends. In a recent reappraisal of Booth's model, Korthals Altes (2014, 29–30) uses the term "negotiation" to describe this back-and-forth between the values implicit in fiction and those shared by audience members.[5] Through interpretation, readers, viewers, or players identify the ethical values that are staged by a fictional work—its ethos, in Aristotle's terminology. Negotiation refers to the way in which these values come into contact with the audience's worldview and moral assumptions, which is a complex process with numerous possible outcomes (depending on both the text and the reader).

Hannah Meretoja, who shares Korthals Altes's focus on interpretation and hermeneutics, highlights a particular outcome of negotiation: for Meretoja, literature "functions as a medium of thought and imagination in which ethical questions are explored in their complexity and messiness, often offering radically new perspectives on them but no definitive answers" (2018, 28). The key word here is "exploration": the negotiation of ethical issues through fiction doesn't produce "definitive answers" but allows audiences to gain new perspectives on ethical dilemmas and conflicts. Instead of affording resolution, narrative negotiation enables audiences to contemplate a clash of values without rushing to conclusions by advocating a pre-existing moral system. This type of negotiation gives readers (viewers, players, etc.) pause, allowing them to take in the multiple—and frequently conflicting—facets of an ethically fraught situation. This process can be emotionally unsettling but also promises to deepen moral reflection through increased awareness of the complexity of the issue at hand. Importantly, Meretoja isn't claiming that this negotiation is the only way in which fiction can engage with ethical questions; but it is the most significant intervention fiction can make in the moral domain precisely by virtue of its open-endedness, a position that also inspires my discussion in this chapter.

Without using the language of negotiation per se, philosopher Cora Diamond (2003) captures a similar clash of values under the heading of the "difficulty of reality." She argues that literature represents a unique means of describing situations in which the mind is unable "to encompass something which it encounters" (2003, 2), with examples from both poetry (Ted Hughes) and prose (J. M. Coetzee). Here I will focus on the latter example. In Coetzee's novella *The Lives of Animals* (1999), the (fictional) writer Elizabeth Costello delivers a lecture on human values in which she draws a comparison between the Holocaust and the large-scale killing of animals in the meat industry. The incendiary parallel is, for Diamond, an example of the difficulty of reality in that it derives from an irresolvable clash of moral intuitions (the defining human tragedy of the twentieth century versus the scale of nonhuman death that human societies are willing to accept, almost without noticing it). Moreover, Costello's admission of the limits of her analogy plays into that sense of difficulty. It is because the parallel fails to advance a well-formed philosophical argument that the difficulty of reality comes to the fore: "Coetzee gives us a view of a profound disturbance of soul, and puts that view into a complex context. What is done by doing so he cannot tell us, he does not know" (Diamond 2003, 11). This idea echoes Meretoja's insight that fiction cannot formulate answers to ethical dilemmas but rather negotiates them by crystallizing their complexity—that is, by revealing the stratification of (possibly opposed or contradictory) emotional and cultural meanings. Indeed, in Coetzee's novella, Costello's predicament reveals tensions and contradictions in the way in which Western societies relate to the lives of nonhuman animals, without resolving such tensions and contradictions. That is the kind of ethical questioning that Coetzee conducts by staging a complex situation of "disturbance of soul."

It is important to note that, while Diamond makes frequent references to moral philosophy in her discussion, her reading of Coetzee's novella foregrounds its affective dimension (including Costello's own emotional states and the audience's responses to her lecture) in addition to ethical values. The implication is that affective experience and ethical values are closely bound up: emotions are a route into the difficulty of reality, not in the sense that they can always help us adjudicate ethical questions, but because they lend a concrete, experiential form to the difficulty of reality theorized by Diamond.[6] Of course, Coetzee's novella negotiates that difficulty through its own literary means, whereas video games have a range of audiovisual and textual strategies as well as interactive mechanics at their disposal. In the next section, I turn to how games probe the complexity of ethical problems, prompting a negotiation of values and evoking the difficulty of reality in the process.

Introducing Ethical Gameplay

The ethical issues that surround video games have attracted a good deal of scholarly attention over the last two decades.[7] Morality is involved in games at multiple levels. Conceptions of right and wrong behavior can be explicitly embedded in game mechanics, for instance through the "moral alignment" system that many role-playing games derive from *Dungeons & Dragons*:

when creating a new character, players choose where they fall on a spectrum that goes from good to evil, a decision that influences their options as they progress through the game. In other games, the player-character's morality isn't a matter of personality but a result of actions taken in the course of each playthrough. In *Red Dead Redemption 2* (Rockstar Games 2018), for example, the player-character's morality isn't a given (as it is in *D&D*-inspired games) but rather depends on whether players engage in altruistic or destructive behavior, based on what the game calls an "honor" system. In games set in the *Star Wars* universe, the choice between the dark side and the light side of the Force fulfills a similar function, suggesting that ethics is fundamentally binary—a choice between good and evil, honor and dishonor, light and dark.

However, these explicit morality systems are only one of the many ways in which gaming practices implicate ethical values. Because games aren't purely abstract systems but represent situations we recognize through real-life experience, players will tend to attach ethical significance to their actions regardless of whether such significance is spelled out by in-game systems. An unprovoked attack on a friendly NPC in *Red Dead Redemption 2* feels wrong even if the game doesn't detract honor points; this doesn't mean that players will always refrain from such seemingly immoral behavior: on the contrary, many will enjoy the transgression, but the very fact that this registers as a transgression shows that ethical and social norms are still part and parcel of the player's experience.[8] In short, games negotiate ethical issues—much like novels and films—through the back-and-forth between the player's worldview and the implicit morality (or "ethos," to use again Booth's Aristotelian terminology) they embed.

Lastly, there is the level of how games may affect readers' moral reasoning, and here psychologists have spent considerable time evaluating—and, largely, debunking—the claim that violence in video games may increase antisocial, aggressive behavior (see, e.g., Przybylski and Weinstein 2019). Game scholars have discussed this impact in broader and more positive terms, positing that a certain kind of gameplay may enhance or deepen players' ethical meaning making. The editors of a 2019 special issue phrase this point as follows: "There is a persistent hope that, by virtue of their interactivity, games can present a very different, and perhaps more powerful, type of ethical engagement than other art forms" (M. Ryan, Formosa, and Tulloch 2019, 300).

The most sustained philosophical discussion of ethical engagement with games to date can be found in Miguel Sicart's (2009, 2013) work. A philosopher and game scholar by training, Sicart also takes his cue from Booth's discussion of ethics in fiction but considers the unique challenges raised by games as an interactive medium. The result, as we will see, is remarkably convergent with the ethics of complexity I have begun to articulate in the previous section through Meretoja's and Diamond's arguments. Sicart's theory of ethical gameplay, as formulated in his 2013 study (but with roots in his 2009 book), centers on the tension between game rules and moral norms; while the former are hardwired into a game system, moral norms are loose and therefore open to interpretation: "Humans follow them even though no authoritative judges preside over them. This leads to a wiggle space where there is the possibility of contextual negotiation and interpretation of these rules" (2013, 8). The flexibility of moral norms, Sicart continues, "allows players to inhabit [game] space with their values while they interpret the conditions of the space by selectively adopting the values proposed by the game as relevant to that experience" (2013, 15). Sicart is theorizing about a particular kind of encounter between an ethically minded player and a game that is designed to raise ethical issues: not all players will pay attention to ethical issues (some may ignore the ethical dimension of games entirely), but those who do stand to benefit from the negotiation—not in terms of moral lessons learned but rather through heightened awareness of the values involved in everyday moral reasoning. In some cases, this awareness may even result in a revision of how these values are applied (or understood) in real-life experience.

Of course, as a game scholar, Sicart is interested in how this type of ethical experience may be afforded by concrete game mechanics or representational devices—how it may be "designed for," as he puts it (2013, 108). Here he draws a distinction between the semiotic layer of games—the situations and characters they represent by way of semiotic cues—and the rules or mechanics from which the interactive experience of gameplay arises. In many cases, the combination of semiotic representation and gameplay rules creates what Sicart calls "cognitive friction" (2013, 93), which is an important source of ethical engagement in video game experiences. As an example of the kind of friction Sicart has in mind, consider the intro sequence of the point-and-click adventure game *The Last Door* (The Game Kitchen 2013): the game starts in the attic of an old house, with the player being in control of a male character clad in nineteenth-century clothes. To advance the game, the player must move a chair toward the center of the room, hang a rope from the ceiling, and finally click on the chair so that the character can put his neck through the noose and commit suicide. The sequence implicates the player uncomfortably in the character's suicide, paving the way for the dark, Poesque atmosphere of the game. In terms of gameplay, we are solving a puzzle by clicking on certain items in a fixed sequence (and note that this is the *only* possible outcome of the scene). Representationally, however, we are enabling suicide. This scene is so unsettling because it builds on the friction between the limited affordances of gameplay and its representational meaning: the ethical stakes of the player's actions emerge from this friction.[9]

This example from *The Last Door* is mine, not Sicart's, but it has the advantage of capturing one of the main takeaways of Sicart's account of ethical gameplay: while the discussion of morality in games has tended to focus on players' *choices* (act honorably or dishonorably, embrace the light or the dark side of the Force, etc.), games may actually be at their most stimulating in ethical terms when they take agency *away* from the player, by presenting them with limited options or undesirable (and unforeseen) consequences. In the case of *The Last Door*, we want to prevent suicide rather than help the character kill himself, but we have no means of doing so; the only way of advancing the game is through the character's death. The kind of cognitive dissonance or friction created by this setup is what gives players pause, encouraging them to reflect on the ethical significance of gameplay. Sicart discusses this type of situation as a "wicked problem," a concept emerging from the social sciences (Rittel and Webber 1973). A wicked problem is, simply enough, a complex situation that doesn't admit of easy solutions—or at least no ethically desirable solutions. In fact, in the case of *The Last Door* the solution is readily available as a sequence of clicks (chair, rope, and again chair). But the wickedness of the problem at hand derives from the fact that, evidently, this solution raises ethical questions, and yet there is no other available option—hence the player's hesitation. Uncertainty is a central dimension of wicked problems in game design: the uncertainty in *The Last Door* is short-lived, since the player realizes right away where this action sequence is going, but games can stretch the uncertainty of consequences and use it to create even more wicked problems.[10]

Through the interplay of game rules and representation, games are well-positioned to probe the complexity of ethical issues that present no "ideal" outcome but only compromises that require the player's (more or less unwilling) complicity.[11] These wicked problems in gameplay thus offer a perspective on Diamond's difficulty of reality. They also illustrate the argument developed by Meretoja: the most important way in which fiction can engage with (or negotiate) ethical values is by foregrounding complexity and messiness, not by imparting clear-cut moral lessons. In the next sections, I will examine three aspects of Soulsring experience that disrupt binary thinking about ethical issues, creating instead a sense of moral murkiness and uncertainty. Players are thus invited to question their moral assumptions, including the assumption (derived from more conventional forms of fantasy) that it is always possible to differentiate pro-social from antisocial behavior. The aspects I will focus on are the NPC quest lines, the games' endings, and the recurring trope of the poison swamp, which I will read as a spatial allegory of the player's ethical complicity in Soulsring games.

The Ethics of Preparing to Cry

When one talks about the difficulty of *DS* or *ER*, the mind immediately goes to the games' notoriously challenging enemies and boss encounters. But ethical difficulties emerge repeatedly in game experience, particularly in conjunction with the side characters the player encounters along the way. I have already discussed in chapters 1 and 2 how, in a typical playthrough, players will run into the same NPC multiple times as they progress through the game world:

these side quests are advanced simply by talking to an NPC or by fulfilling their requests (retrieving certain objects, killing an enemy, and so on). When these conditions are met (and they vary from NPC to NPC), the character will move to the next location, and they will keep moving until the end of the quest line, following the player's own journey through the game world. The process can be remarkably obscure, since there is no easy way of tracking the NPCs' requests or current location. Further, the player is often in the dark as to the consequences of their actions and how they may affect *other* NPCs, an uncertainty that as we will see creates a sense of moral difficulty. Frequently, and somewhat counterintuitively, these quest lines result in the NPCs' death.[12] This is counterintuitive because role-playing games tend to cast the protagonist in the role of hero-helper, with the side quests providing tangible rewards (through special items or experience points) for their altruistic behavior. In Soulsring games, however, the player's altruism tends to backfire; NPCs are consistently worse off after the player-character's intervention than beforehand. This result suggests that it is often impossible in Soulsring worlds to neatly distinguish between ethically desirable and undesirable actions: instead, the player is immersed in a universe of ethical uncertainty that resonates with, and expands, the difficulty built into gameplay.

In *ER*, Boc the Seamster is a case in point: as seen in chapter 3, Boc asks the player-character for a special item known as a "larval tear" in order to be reborn and overcome his animal form, which he characterizes as "ugly." If the player decides to deliver this larval tear, however, Boc metamorphoses into a human being and dies shortly thereafter. In hindsight, we realize that Boc himself had predicted this fate by asking the player-character: "Must I be reborn, no matter what ill fate awaits me?" Unwittingly, then, the player becomes complicit in this "ill fate," even as they thought they were merely helping Boc by fulfilling his request. The character's death isn't strictly inevitable, though, unlike what happens in the suicide sequence from *The Last Door*. However, the alternative (using a special item to convince Boc that he isn't ugly) is so convoluted that very few players will know how to unlock it, unless they resort to an online guide or engage in a time-consuming trial-and-error process. Even if the player does manage to prevent Boc's death, the reward is limited: because the NPC doesn't die, he can continue to alter the player's armor, but these are mostly cosmetic alterations with limited impact on gameplay.

The *DS* series also offers many examples of quest lines that go awry when completed. One of the most likable characters in *DS3* is the heavily armored warrior Siegward. We encounter this NPC a number of times, establishing a mutually supportive relationship as we go: we retrieve his armor (stolen by the trickster Patches, a recurring character throughout Soulsring games) and help him out of a well in the Cathedral of the Deep; he assists us in a several boss fights and prepares a restorative soup for us—a rare moment of downtime in a game full of tense situations. This quest line accompanies us for most of the game, right until a fight against the boss known as Yhorm the Giant, to which Siegward inevitably succumbs. Lore-focused YouTuber VaatiVidya explains that Siegward's death is the final act in a family saga that started in the first *DS* game with a character (Siegmeyer) who wears an onion-shaped armor identical to Siegward's.[13] The video belongs to VaatiVidya's popular "Prepare to Cry" series, which explores the backstories of NPCs like Siegward but also some of the game's bosses. As the name suggests, the video series probes the emotional depth of Soulsring lore, which favors round characters with surprising and frequently unfortunate backstories: the episode devoted to Siegmeyer and Siegward turns their stories into a family tragedy of sorts, with Siegward in *DS3* facing the same dark fate as his ancestor in *DS1*.

The inevitability of Siegward's death, which re-enacts the earlier death of Siegmeyer, can be understood in light of George Steiner's (2004) conceptualization of tragedy. Steiner explains that the tragic condition turns the protagonist into "an unwelcome guest of life or, at best, a threatened stranger on this hostile or indifferent earth" (2004, 2). Siegward's death embodies this hostility; his previous courteousness toward the player-character—his being an impeccable "host" during the restorative soup scene—throws the unwelcomeness he experiences into sharp relief. The repetitive pattern created by Siegmeyer's and Siegward's deaths further amplifies this tragic element, as VaatiVidya's "Prepare to Cry" video articulates with exceptional lucidity. Moreover, Siegward's fate is not only a matter of narrative representation (the curse of Siegmeyer's family) but deeply implicates the player through their inability to prevent Siegward's demise on the level of gameplay.

The ending of that quest line offers a substantial reward in gameplay terms, because Siegward drops his distinctively shaped armor set, which is one of the best in the game. But that reward must be weighed against the tragic emotions generated by the events in which players find themselves complicit, and complicit in a way that they could not have foreseen. The fact that players *cannot* take the moral high ground (by preventing Siegward's death and thus refusing the reward of his armor) muddles their ethical calculus. Instead, players must face the fact that game narrative involves lending help and causing harm at the same time, and often to the same NPCs. In that respect, players' dilemma is not unlike that of many *DS* and *ER* villains: flawed creatures who, as VaatiVidya's "Prepare to Cry" videos reconstruct in detail, are frequently divided between altruistic and destructive impulses.[14] Ethical complexity is thus at the heart of Soulsring quest lines, positioning the player-character (and by extension the player) as deeply and uncertainly implicated in a world that resists simple moral judgments.

Multiple Endings and Open Questions

Typically, we expect the ending to lend closure to the narrative by resolving the instabilities and complications introduced by the plot earlier on.[15] While of course not all narratives offer the same degree of closure, a plot is not complete without a retrospective vantage point for evaluating its significance, which is precisely what the ending is supposed to provide. Also in moral terms, the ending gives definitive shape to the ethical values negotiated by the story, exerting considerable influence on the audience's moral meaning making. Soulsring games, like many other narrative-focused games, feature multiple endings, largely reflecting the player's choices after the final boss fight and typically also in earlier interactions. The availability of an ending depends on whether the player has pursued the quest lines of certain NPCs *before* getting to the game's final encounter. However, not all Soulsring games are identical in this respect, because endings have become more and more complicated in the course of the *DS* series, with *ER* offering the most intricate ending experience. What has not changed, as I will show in the next pages, is their foregrounding of ethical ambivalence.

Let us start with *DS1*. As I stated at the beginning of the chapter, the *DS* universe is based on a distinction between Fire and Dark, which *could* be interpreted as a moral dichotomy between good and evil but in fact resists any straightforward ethical evaluation. The Age of Fire is coming to an end, and it is up to the player to decide whether it should be extended or whether the First Flame should be allowed to die out, ushering in a new Age of Dark. This is, essentially, the function of the ending of *DS1*: after defeating Gwyn, the player is given the chance to rekindle the First Flame and thus extend the Age of Fire. As the final cutscene makes clear, the player-character immolates themselves in the Flame, thus becoming Gwyn's successor as the Lord of Cinder. Alternatively, the player can walk away from the Flame, which goes out, thus marking the beginning of the Age of Dark and turning the player into a Dark Lord.

The choice is binary, but the morality that underlies these endings is not; this is revealed in dialogue with two Primordial Serpents (Frampt and Kaathe) encountered earlier on in the playthrough, whose role is to coax the player into the "Fire" and "Dark" ending, respectively. The player may decide to side with Frampt and give up their own life to extend the Age of Fire, but it is unclear that doing so accomplishes anything, since the Flame is destined to fade sooner or later. This isn't saving the world so much as preserving the status quo, including the Undead Curse that is afflicting humanity (whatever "humanity" means in the world of *DS*—see the discussion in chapter 3). On the other hand, the Age of Dark promises to be an "age of men," as Kaathe suggests, but we can't be certain that putting humans in charge will be enough to counter the Curse.[16]

The player who chooses to do Frampt's bidding and extend the Age of Fire is, ultimately, being manipulated by primordial forces beyond their control—and, largely, beyond their comprehension. In that sense, this ending is yet another manifestation of the ludic sublime theorized by Vella (2015). If players choose to follow Kaathe's advice, by contrast, the "Dark" ending promises to bring about genuine change in the game world, possibly ending the Undead Curse and therefore also humanity's subjugation at the hands of Lords of Cinder like Gwyn. This prospect seems to run counter to the negative connotations of darkness, but we are never told whether all this pans out. It remains unclear whether releasing humanity from hollowing (see chapter 3) leads to any improvement in their situation.

The beginning of *DS2*, which closely mirrors the setup of *DS1*, suggests that the player's choice to end the Age of Fire may not matter at all, since Fire and Dark seem to be locked in an eternal cycle. In short, both *DS1* endings position the player within a moral gray zone: they cue ideas of good and evil but make it impossible for players to ascribe unambiguous moral significance. As VaatiVidya puts it, "Most games either have one canon ending or allow you to choose from a selection of moral minefield endings at the end of the game. *Dark Souls* is the latter but the endings are ambiguous as hell. The more you learn about the game, the more confusing the endings become."[17]

The next installments in the *DS* series amplify the confusion by introducing mechanical complications to the binary ending of *DS1*. The starting point of *DS2* is that the world is locked in a cycle of Fire and Dark (see chapter 1 for more on this cyclicity), which also shows that the choice we made at the end of the previous game is irrelevant. If the player advances to the end of *DS2* without defeating an optional boss named King Vendrick, only one ending is available: the player-character takes the Throne of Want, which essentially means perpetuating the cycle of Fire and Dark. If, however, the player has beaten Vendrick and talked to Aldia, a blob-like creature that appears at key moments in the game's progression, then a second ending opens up: the player can walk away from the Throne of Want. This ending is superficially similar to the Dark ending of *DS1* (in which the player decides not to link the fire) but suggests something profoundly different: the binary of Fire and Dark is rejected, and instead the player is seeking an alternative, a way past this binary that would also put an end to the Undead Curse. This alternative may seem like a more desirable outcome than the Fire-Dark cycle; it promises to overcome the binary created by *DS1*, but the promise is never fulfilled (even if the game's DLCs or expansions go some way toward fleshing it out). Significantly, the second ending becomes available only if the player has taken certain actions in the course of the playthrough, a device that both encourages replay and rewards players who have taken on a challenging optional boss.

DS3 builds on the same recipe but makes the third ending even more mechanically difficult to achieve. The basic choice here is, again, between rekindling the First Flame and letting it die out, but for the latter ending to become available the player has to complete a number of interactions with an important NPC, the Fire Keeper. The third ending, known as the "usurpation" ending, is unlocked by taking a much longer series of steps as part of Yoel of Londor's quest line. This sequence is far more complicated than gaining access to the third ending of *DS2*: players may be locked out of this ending simply because they forgot to talk to a certain NPC at the right time during the playthrough. At first sight, we may think that the difficulty of achieving this third ending increases its ethical desirability, and indeed the usurpation ending does raise hopes that the Fire-Dark cycle may be broken and humanity may be saved from hollowing. But, as in the case of *DS2*, it is debatable whether this third, more convoluted ending can be considered the "good" one. The final cutscene, with a horde of hollows bowing in front of the player-character (now Lord of Hollows), certainly doesn't project much optimism (see figure 6.1). As a *DS3* player remarks on Reddit, referencing one of the locations visited by the player-character in *DS2* (Oolacile): "I would hardly consider an ending where you let Anri be assassinated and then desecrate her corpse a good ending. Also keep in mind what's been happening to the hollows and what happened to the people of Oolacile. There is no promise of salvation from the curse substantiated in your becoming king of a bunch of walking corpses on the brink of mutation and insanity."[18] In short, the difficulty of reaching a certain ending doesn't guarantee that it will solve the ethical uncertainty at the heart of *DS* series: the two endings in *DS2* and *DS3* that challenge the basic binary setup by *DS1* can be superficially understood as more ethically desirable, but they fail to bring genuine closure to the *DS* universe, as the debate on Reddit attests.

ER adopts a similar template, but on a much larger scale, in keeping with its vast open world. Six endings are on offer here, but their availability depends on which quest lines the player has followed in the course of their playthrough. The first of these endings requires no secondary quest lines: the player embraces the Greater Will, choosing to mend the Elden Ring

Figure 6.1 A screenshot from the usurpation ending in *Dark Souls 3*, with the player-character in the foreground.

and become the new Elden Lord. Three more endings are a variation on this "default" ending but require special "Mending Runes" that can be collected through NPC quests: these runes give the ending a slightly different flavor and atmosphere, either by perfecting the Golden Order imposed by the Greater Will or by changing it permanently. The player-character is still the Elden Lord, but the nature of the world they rule over changes considerably: Death is inscribed into the Golden Order (the ending unlocked by Fia's quest), or a new curse takes over (the conclusion to the Dung Eater's quest). Essentially, these endings work analogously to linking the fire in *DS* games: a precarious order is extended, but it is unclear how long it will last or what (if any) benefit the world's tarnished inhabitants will receive from it.

The last two endings—the Lord of Frenzied Flame and the Age of Stars—break with the Golden Order, ushering in an age of chaos or, alternatively, an age under the sign of the Dark Moon, as envisioned by Ranni the Witch (one of the game's main NPCs).[19] *ER* players have debated the significance of these endings extensively, and the two endings that oppose the Golden Order are typically singled out as the most rewarding ones from a plot perspective. They are also the most complicated ones to achieve. Nevertheless, the difficulty of triggering a certain ending is no guarantee of moral desirability: if re-establishing the Greater Will does nothing but extend the world's status quo, the Frenzied Flame and the Age of Stars endings promise a new beginning but offer no indication that the new world will be a happier place than it was before the player's actions.[20]

Throughout *DS* and *ER*, our ethical meaning making is stimulated by the existence of multiple endings, with some of them being much more difficult to realize than others; but the ambiguity that surrounds all of these endings disrupts the community's ability to identify or agree on the most satisfying one from a moral standpoint. Far from being a flaw, however, the absence of an unequivocally good ending is what enables ethical gameplay, inviting players to reflect on how FromSoftware games tend to stage morally fraught situations (wicked problems) with no ideal outcomes. The resulting complexity, which is irresolvable, proves generative rather than paralyzing: it affords players the opportunity to share and compare their ethical evaluations, in a process that extends the complexity of game experience to the intersubjective context of (for instance) a Reddit thread, as seen in the previous chapter. The difficulty of gameplay, including the difficulty of reaching a certain ending, thus goes hand in hand with the moral difficulty experienced by players as they attempt to work through the ethical values involved in the endings.

Allegorical Swamps

FromSoftware games feature a number of returning locations, including the undead town, the library or archive, and the castle. Judging by discussions on Reddit and other internet platforms, the most dreaded of these locations is undoubtedly the poison swamp, which appears under the following names: Blighttown (*DS1*), Black Gulch and Harvest Valley (*DS2*), Farron Keep (*DS3*), and the Swamp of Aeonia and the Lake of Rot (*ER*). These poison swamps differ in terms of size and visual properties, but they tend to have two features in common: they slow down the player-character's movement, making it more difficult to traverse the terrain than anywhere else in Soulsring worlds; and they poison the player, causing a slow loss of health points unless certain protective measures are taken, mostly involving the use of rare or costly items to counter the effects of the poison. The result increases the already considerable difficulty of the games' combat, because the player must keep track of and manage health loss from poison in addition to the damage dealt by the enemies directly. The unpopularity of these areas is hardly surprising, then. Miyazaki himself declared in an interview: "I know how people feel about [poison swamps] … but you know, suddenly I realize I'm in the middle of making one and I just can't help myself. It just happens" (quoted in McWhertor 2022).

To conclude this chapter on ethics, I want to suggest that poison swamps don't just "happen" in Soulsring games but serve an important allegorical function: they offer a human-scale, embodied equivalent to the ethical difficulty that emerges from various aspects of the game world and narrative, and they blend that difficulty with the considerable challenges of gameplay. Miyazaki's poison swamps reflect a cultural understanding of wetlands that stretches back at least to Dante's *Divine Comedy*, where the Styx (a river of Greco-Roman mythology) is presented as a marsh surrounding the fifth circle of hell. Commenting on Dante's marsh as well as the "Slough of Despond" of John Bunyan's *The Pilgrim's Progress*, Anthony Wilson argues that swamps often "become a metaphor for man's moral shortcomings, the physical analogue for the morass of sin in which the mortal traveller risks becoming lost" (2018, 114). The notion of moral corruption is certainly present in Soulsring games as well; particularly in *ER*, many of the bosses appear to be diminished or tainted versions of their past selves. However, *DS* games and *ER* offer a reinterpretation of the swamp based on the unavailability of the Christian morality orienting Dante's and Bunyan's poetic worlds: here, the stickiness of the swamp doesn't signal distance from God as the ultimate arbiter of moral questions but rather suggests the inseparability of the player-character from a condition of moral ambiguity or precarity.

I have already introduced the image schema of entanglement in chapter 1 to discuss the nonlinear organization of Soulsring quest lines. By slowing down the player-character's progress and draining their health pools (thus making the game even more difficult), the swamps also evoke the schema of entanglement: the player-character is physically caught up in FromSoftware's poison swamps. Further, the poison swamps offer an allegorical perspective on a different type of entanglement that traverses the games—namely, the player's implication in situations whose ethical stakes are ambiguous, unclear, or unresolved. This reading builds on the tendency to refer to complexity (particularly, but not exclusively, in the ethical domain) as a "morass," "quagmire," or a situation in which one gets "bogged down"—all variations on the swamp as a place of sticky and dangerous connection, which keeps us from drawing sharp distinctions between right and wrong. The poison swamp thus condenses the affective and ethical difficulty at the heart of all Soulsring games—the way in which players are entangled in a world that raises numerous ethical questions and offers few answers.

Thus, while in literature like Dante's or Bunyan's works the swamp functions in opposition to a place of moral certainty, *DS* and *ER* use the swamp to amplify the moral treacherousness that defines the game world as a whole. The slowness of the player's progression through the poison swamps becomes an embodied allegory for the way in which the games destabilize the binary morality of the fantasy genre, either by implicating the player-character—unpredictably—in the life and death of NPCs or by presenting them with a number of highly ambiguous or open endings. Since the swamps also increase the already considerable difficulty of gameplay (as noted by the many players who dread this recurring location), the allegorical entanglement extends to the challenges created by game design: this space thus brings together implication in the murky morality of the game world and the mechanical difficulty of gameplay.

***

Like other media, video games are capable of bringing up and negotiating a broad gamut of ethical issues. Negotiation is not the same as delivering moral lessons or imposing a pre-existing value system, however: on the contrary, scholars have suggested that the best way to think about fiction is as an open-ended "moral laboratory"—to use Hakemulder's (2000) terminology—that stimulates the audience's ethical meaning making while allowing them to reach their own conclusions. The foregrounding of ethically complex or difficult situations is an important means of creating space for ethical reflection. Seen through the safe distance of fictional representation, the messiness or "wickedness" of moral problems offers an opportunity for reappraising the usual pathways of ethical reasoning and the values it involves. In video games, this negotiation of ethical difficulty is realized through a combination of semiotic, representational cues and the specific affordances of gameplay. Particularly significant in this respect is how games may undermine players' agency, as highlighted by Sicart (2013), in an effort to bring home the unavailability of ethically ideal solutions.

This is precisely the type of engagement that FromSoftware games encourage by entangling the player in situations whose moral stakes are murky or uncertain. I have explored this murkiness by examining two aspects of *DS* games and *ER*: the side quests that revolve around particular NPCs and the endings. The side quests complicate expectations (largely derived from fantasy genre conventions) that the player-character take on the role of a helper and receive rewards for engaging in altruistic behavior. Instead, the side quests have mixed results in terms of impact on the NPCs' lives (which are consistently ruined by the player's well-meaning efforts) and also in terms of gameplay and moral rewards for the player. The tragic nature of the NPCs' stories, underscored by the community through creative content such as VaatiVidya's "Prepare to Cry" video series, immerses the player in a world of deeply uncertain morality.

For their part, the games' endings create moral ambiguity by withholding information on the ramifications of the player's decisions: whether the status quo (the cycle of Fire and Dark in *DS*, the Golden Order in *ER*) is affirmed or challenged, we are given no reassurance that the world after the ending will be less broken than the one we have just plodded through. Players are encouraged to pursue complicated quest lines that unlock new endings, but the work they put into achieving these endings doesn't have a clear moral payoff. Instead, players are left in a moral no man's land that finds a concrete equivalent in the games' infamous poison swamps, which physically obstruct and complicate the player's progression in order to allegorically signal their entanglement in a situation that they cannot fully control. That physical entanglement resonates with the games' negotiation of morally complex scenarios from which players struggle to distance themselves. There is no clear-cut right or wrong in Soulsring worlds, only a troubling sense of complicity with forces that we cannot understand fully. Instead of proving debilitating, however, this complicity generates debate and prompts players to critically interrogate the possibility and limits of ethical meaning making, as the discussion on platforms such as Reddit and YouTube shows.

To circle back to this book's beginning, the difficulty of Soulsring games is never merely mechanical, never a matter of level design or the player-character's health pool alone. This is, incidentally, what many souls-like games fail to capture, despite featuring gameplay situations and bosses that are at least as hard as those of FromSoftware titles. The challenges of combat, in Soulsring games, go hand in hand with the obscurity of the storytelling, and both dimensions of the player's experience feed into a sense of complexity, understood as the stratification of possibly conflicting meanings—hence the moral uncertainty discussed in this chapter.

This book has examined how this complexity—which is on a par with the complexity associated with literary works—emerges across a number of layers of game and narrative design, starting from the basic spatiotemporal coordinates of Soulsring worlds, their nonlinear temporality, and intricate spatial setting. Even the concept of the human becomes unstable, in the games and in the discussion thereof, marking a convergence with contemporary theorizations of the posthuman. Community building is a direct response to the games' complexity, with players comparing notes and joining forces (particularly in lore-focused discussion groups) to work through the gaps left by the storytelling. Because complexity tends to obfuscate or disrupt the negotiation of meaning, Soulsring communities become strikingly self-aware of their interpretive efforts, as my discussion in the penultimate chapter has argued.

Moreover, the games' inherent complexity is responsible for creating moral ambiguity, as I have argued here, and that link between kinesthetic and ethical difficulty might well be the most productive way of conceptualizing the recalcitrance of Soulsring games. These are games that use ludic and narrative means to ask radical questions, inviting players to confront existential insecurities and moral blind spots on both a personal and a cultural level. The games don't settle those questions but leave them open for players to ponder and debate, as this book's engagement with the Soulsring community has suggested. It is beyond the scope of this book to consider what the value of that type of experience might be. If I can speculate in closing, however, I would suggest that the complexity of Soulsring games provides a form of training in uncertainty. It shows players, individually and collectively, how to inhabit a game world where knowledge is partial, defeasible, sometimes even contradictory, and human life—whatever the definition of the human one adopts—fundamentally fragile.

That world resembles ours in many ways, particularly as climate change and various other forms of global upheaval make our outlook on the future more uncertain.[21] I am reminded of the expressions "groundlessness" or "laying down a path in walking," which is how philosophers of mind Francisco Varela, Evan Thompson, and Eleanor Rosch (1991, 237) describe the operations of cognition. The world, from Varela, Thompson, and Rosch's "enactivist" perspective, doesn't pre-exist us as cognitive agents: on the contrary, we create or enact the world on the fly, precariously, as we engage with physical and social environments that cannot be fully known. The cognition of embodied, biological, mortal beings is inherently groundless and precarious, but the system of culture works toward grounding our experience in ideas that look like certainties: religious beliefs, frameworks for morality, or metanarratives of scientific progress and economic growth. Some artifacts within a culture are designed to unsettle those ideas and face us with our groundlessness. Soulsring games might be doing just that, and that is why they are so resonant in times of personal or cultural uncertainty. My discussion of Soulsring games and mental health crises in chapter 5 has come close to that idea.

Of course, only in a speculative leap of faith can one extrapolate from gameplay to real-world experience. I simply do not have the evidence to claim that Soulsring gameplay can help us cope with uncertainty in any statistically generalizable way. But perhaps, on some level, that promise is what keeps players coming back to Soulsring games, for all their daunting difficulties. By constantly reminding players of their limited skills and incomplete understanding of the games' intricate lore, these games cultivate acceptance of the uncertainty of real-life experience; they train us in the art of "staying with the trouble," to lift Donna Haraway's (2016) formulation, which entails acceptance of precarity and vulnerability. Just as importantly, though, Soulsring games highlight community as a way of collectively coming to terms with those uncertainties.

Notes

1 The quotation comes from Raffel (1968, 223).
2 See, for instance, the discussion on this subreddit: https://www.reddit.com/r/darksouls/comments/1jsomi/a_question_of_morality/.
3 For more on the distinction between ethics and morality, see Gert and Gert (2020).
4 Here and throughout this section I use the term "fiction" in a broad sense, as referring to any practice involving make-believe (Walton 1990), including video games. This typically means extending the claims offered by the scholars I engage with, who mostly talk about fiction in a narrow sense (i.e., literary fiction). I will turn to the specificity of video games in the next section.
5 Korthals Altes also refers to Herman and Vervaeck's (2009) discussion of narrative negotiation, which is largely convergent with hers.
6 For more on emotions and ethics, see Hogan (2022, chap. 3).
7 See, e.g., the special issues edited by Capurro et al. (2005) and Ryan et al. (2019), in addition to the work I'll discuss in this section.
8 See Consalvo (2005) on how the concept of "magic circle," derived from Johan Huizinga's (1949) work and frequently invoked in game studies, has led scholars to downplay the circulation of values from the real world to game worlds.
9 For more on the Poesque atmosphere of *The Last Door*, see Caracciolo (2019).
10 See also Costikyan's (2013) account of uncertainty in games. Developing Sicart's model, Bosman (2019) offers a sustained discussion of wicked problems in game experiences.
11 See Sicart: "The response to wicked problems is player complicity. Wicked problems make players complicit in the experience of the game" (2013, 106).
12 See also this video on the NPCs' lives we "ruined by 'helping'" in *ER*: https://youtu.be/IU-yPr5N3Eo.
13 https://youtu.be/297nrC5DWMQ.
14 See this statement by a Reddit user who comments on the emotional impact of the "Prepare to Cry" series: "Realizing that most (all?) of these enemies (or at least the bosses) aren't really evil makes it all so much worse. Most of them are just trying to find their own way, or fix the mistakes of their past, or carve a happy future." https://www.reddit.com/r/darksouls/comments/3xhqc1/prepare_to_cry/.
15 The concepts of "instability" and "complication" play a central role in James Phelan's (2007) rhetorical account of narrative progression as well as earlier structuralist models (e.g., Todorov 1968). For more on closure, see Segal (2010).
16 See here for Kaathe's dialogue lines: https://darksouls.wiki.fextralife.com/Darkstalker+Kaathe.
17 https://youtu.be/RwUm_S1fedw.
18 https://www.reddit.com/r/darksouls3/comments/4fs6la/lore_analysis_the_endings/.
19 For an overview of these endings, see https://eldenring.wiki.fextralife.com/Endings.
20 See, for example, the discussions on this subreddit: https://www.reddit.com/r/Eldenring/comments/tcyxcy/best_ending_in_elden_ring/.
21 More on climate uncertainty and its narrative negotiation in Caracciolo (2022a).

Works Cited

Aarseth, Espen. 1997. *Cybertext*. Baltimore: Johns Hopkins University Press.

———. 2007. "Allegories of Space: The Question of Spatiality in Computer Games." In *Space Time Play: Computer Games, Architecture and Urbanism. The Next Level*, edited by F. von Borries, S. P. Walz, and M. Böttger, 152–71. Berlin: Birkhäuser.

Aarseth, Espen, and Sebastian Möring. 2020. "The Game Itself? Towards a Hermeneutics of Computer Games." In *Proceedings of the 15th International Conference on the Foundations of Digital Games*, 1–8. https://doi.org/10.1145/3402942.3402978.

Abbott, H. Porter. 2008. *The Cambridge Introduction to Narrative*. Cambridge: Cambridge University Press.

———. 2013. *Real Mysteries: Narrative and the Unknowable*. Columbus: Ohio State University Press.

———. 2014. "Narrativity." In *The Living Handbook of Narratology*, edited by Peter Hühn. Hamburg: Hamburg University Press. https://www-archiv.fdm.uni-hamburg.de/lhn/node/27.html.

Alighieri, Dante. 2003. *The Divine Comedy*. Translated by John Ciardi. New York: New American Library.

Arjoranta, Jonne. 2011. "Do We Need Real-Time Hermeneutics? Structures of Meaning in Games." In *Proceedings of the 2011 DiGRA International Conference: Think Design Play*. Utrecht: DiGRA/Utrecht School of the Arts. http://www.digra.org/wp-content/uploads/digital-library/11310.17396.pdf.

Bakhtin, Mikhail. 1984. *Rabelais and His World*. Bloomington: Indiana University Press.

Ballard, Mary Elizabeth, and Kelly Marie Welch. 2017. "Virtual Warfare: Cyberbullying and Cyber-Victimization in MMOG Play." *Games and Culture* 12 (5): 466–91.

Basney, Lionel. 1980. "Tolkien and the Ethical Function of 'Escape' Literature." *Mosaic: A Journal for the Interdisciplinary Study of Literature* 13 (2): 23–36.

Bennett, Rhianna M., Krystiana L. Krupa, Kate Minniti, and Alexander Vandewalle. 2023. "What Lasts of Us: Implicit Archaeology Through Environmental Storytelling." *Journal of Geek Studies* 10 (2): 89–97.

Birke, Dorothee. 2021. "Social Reading? On the Rise of a 'Bookish' Reading Culture Online." *Poetics Today* 42 (2): 149–72.

Boellstorff, Tom, Bonnie Nardi, Celia Pearce, and T. L. Taylor. 2013. *Ethnography and Virtual Worlds*. Princeton, NJ: Princeton University Press.

Bogost, Ian. 2006. *Unit Operations: An Approach to Videogame Criticism*. Cambridge, MA: MIT Press.

Booth, Wayne C. 1988. *The Company We Keep: An Ethics of Fiction*. Berkeley: University of California Press.

Bordwell, David. 2002. "Film Futures." *SubStance* 31 (1): 88–104.

———. 2008. *Poetics of Cinema*. New York: Routledge.

Boroditsky, Lera. 2000. "Metaphoric Structuring: Understanding Time through Spatial Metaphors." *Cognition* 75 (1): 1–28.

Bosman, Frank G. 2019. "There Is No Solution!: 'Wicked Problems' in Digital Games." *Games and Culture* 14 (5): 543–59.

Boyer, Pascal. 2002. *Religion Explained: The Human Instincts That Fashion Gods, Spirits and Ancestors*. New York: Basic Books.

Braidotti, Rosi. 2013. *The Posthuman*. Cambridge: Polity Press.

Buckland, Warren. 2009a. "Introduction: Puzzle Plots." In *Puzzle Films: Complex Storytelling in Contemporary Cinema*, edited by Warren Buckland, 1–12. Chichester: Wiley-Blackwell.

———, ed. 2009b. *Puzzle Films: Complex Storytelling in Contemporary Cinema*. Chichester: Wiley-Blackwell.

Callus, Ivan, Stefan Herbrechter, and Manuela Rossini. 2014. "Introduction: Dis/Locating Posthumanism in European Literary and Critical Traditions." *European Journal of English Studies* 18 (2): 103–20.

Campbell, Joseph. 1949. *The Hero with a Thousand Faces*. Princeton, NJ: Princeton University Press.

Capurro, Rafael, Thomas Hausmanninger, Karsten Weber, and Felix Weil, eds. 2005. "Ethics of E-Games." *The International Review of Information Ethics* 4. https://informationethics.ca/index.php/irie/article/view/173.

Caracciolo, Marco. 2014. "Interpretation for the Bodies: Bridging the Gap." *Style* 48 (3): 385–403.

———. 2015. "Playing *Home*: Video Game Experiences Between Narrative and Ludic Interests." *Narrative* 23 (3): 231–51.

———. 2016. "Cognitive Literary Studies and the Status of Interpretation: An Attempt at Conceptual Mapping." *New Literary History* 47 (3): 187–208.

———. 2019. "Edgar Allan Poe Simulators: On Dream Logic, Game Narratives, and Poesque Atmospheres." In *Intermedia Games—Games Inter Media: Video Games and Intermediality*, edited by Michael Fuchs and Jeff Thoss, 167–88. New York: Bloomsbury.

———. 2021. *Narrating the Mesh: Form and Story in the Anthropocene*. Charlottesville: University of Virginia Press.

———. 2022a. *Contemporary Fiction and Climate Uncertainty: Narrating Unstable Futures*. New York: Bloomsbury.

———. 2022b. "Materiality, Nonlinearity, and Interpretive Openness in Contemporary Archaeogames." *Eludamos: Journal for Computer Game Culture* 13 (1): 29–47.

———. 2022c. "Remediating Video Games in Contemporary Fiction: Literary Form and Intermedial Transfer." *Games and Culture* 18 (5): 664–83.

Caracciolo, Marco, and Shannon Lambert. 2019. "Narrative Bodies and Nonhuman Transformations." *SubStance* 48 (3): 45–63.

Carroll, Noël. 2003. "The Grotesque Today: Preliminary Notes Toward a Taxonomy." In *Modern Art and the Grotesque*, edited by Frances S. Connelly, 291–312. Cambridge: Cambridge University Press.

Carruth, Shane, dir. 2004. *Primer*. THINKFilm.

CD Projekt RED. 2015. *The Witcher 3: Wild Hunt.* Microsoft Windows.

Chang, Alenda Y. 2019. *Playing Nature: Ecology in Video Games.* Minneapolis: University of Minnesota Press.

Chatman, Seymour. 1978. *Story and Discourse.* Ithaca, NY: Cornell University Press.

Christie, Deborah, and Sarah Juliet Lauro, eds. 2011. *Better Off Dead: The Evolution of the Zombie as Post-Human.* New York: Fordham University Press.

Ciccoricco, David. 2007. "'Play, Memory': *Shadow of the Colossus* and Cognitive Workouts." *Dichtung-Digital* 37: 1–13. https://doi.org/10.25969/mediarep/17705.

———. 2016. "Digital Culture and Posthumanism." In *The Cambridge History of Postmodern Literature,* edited by Brian McHale and Len Platt, 419–33. Cambridge: Cambridge University Press.

Clarke, Bruce. 2008. *Posthuman Metamorphosis: Narrative and Systems.* New York: Fordham University Press.

Coetzee, J. M. 1999. *The Lives of Animals.* Princeton, NJ: Princeton University Press.

Colombetti, Giovanna. 2013. *The Feeling Body: Affective Science Meets the Enactive Mind.* Cambridge, MA: MIT Press.

Consalvo, Mia. 2005. "Rule Sets, Cheating, and Magic Circles: Studying Games and Ethics." *The International Review of Information Ethics* 4: 7–12.

———. 2012. "Confronting Toxic Gamer Culture: A Challenge for Feminist Game Studies Scholars." *Ada: A Journal of Gender, New Media, and Technology* 1. https://doi.org/10.7264/N33X84KH.

———. 2022. *Atari to Zelda: Japan's Videogames in Global Contexts.* Cambridge, MA: MIT Press.

Costikyan, Greg. 2013. *Uncertainty in Games.* Cambridge, MA: MIT Press.

Czachesz, István. 2009. "Metamorphosis and Mind: Cognitive Explorations of the Grotesque in Early Christian Literature." In *Metamorphoses: Resurrection, Body and Transformative Practices in Early Christianity,* edited by Turid Karlsen Seim and Jorunn Økland, 207–30. Berlin: De Gruyter.

D'Anastasio, Cecilia. 2021. "*D&D* Must Grapple With the Racism in Fantasy." *Wired.* https://www.wired.com/story/dandd-must-grapple-with-the-racism-in-fantasy/.

Daston, Lorraine, and Glenn W. Most. 2015. "History of Science and History of Philologies." *Isis* 106 (2): 378–90.

Diamond, Cora. 2003. "The Difficulty of Reality and the Difficulty of Philosophy." *Partial Answers* 1 (2): 1–26.

Eco, Umberto. 1989. *The Open Work.* Translated by Anna Cancogni. Cambridge, MA: Harvard University Press.

Elsaesser, Thomas. 2009. "The Mind-Game Film." In *Puzzle Films: Complex Storytelling in Contemporary Cinema,* edited by Warren Buckland, 13–41. Chichester: Wiley-Blackwell.

Ensslin, Astrid. 2014. *Literary Gaming.* Cambridge, MA: MIT Press.

Eskelinen, Markku. 2001. "The Gaming Situation." *Game Studies* 1 (1). http://www.gamestudies.org/0101/eskelinen/.

Ferguson, Christopher J., Cheryl K. Olson, Lawrence A. Kutner, and Dorothy E. Warner. 2014. "Violent Video Games, Catharsis Seeking, Bullying, and Delinquency: A Multivariate Analysis of Effects." *Crime & Delinquency* 60 (5): 764–84.

Fernández-Vara, Clara. 2011. "Game Spaces Speak Volumes: Indexical Storytelling." In *Proceedings of the 2011 DiGRA International Conference: Think Design Play.*

Utrecht: DiGRA/Utrecht School of the Arts. http://www.digra.org/wp-content/uploads/digital-library/Game-Spaces-Speak-Volumes.pdf.

Fialho, Olivia. 2019. "What Is Literature for? The Role of Transformative Reading." *Cogent Arts & Humanities* 6 (1): 1–16.

Fish, Stanley. 1980. *Is There a Text in This Class? The Authority of Interpretive Communities*. Cambridge, MA: Harvard University Press.

Fox, Jesse, Michael Gilbert, and Wai Yen Tang. 2018. "Player Experiences in a Massively Multiplayer Online Game: A Diary Study of Performance, Motivation, and Social Interaction." *New Media & Society* 20 (11): 4056–73.

Frasca, Gonzalo. 2003a. "Simulation versus Narrative: Introduction to Ludology." In *The Video Game Theory Reader*, edited by Mark J. P. Wolf and Bernard Perron, 221–35. New York: Routledge.

———. 2003b. "Ludologists Love Stories, Too: Notes from a Debate That Never Took Place." In *Level Up*, edited by Marinka Copier and Joost Raessens. Utrecht: University of Utrecht. http://www.digra.org/dl/db/05163.01125.

FromSoftware. 2009. *Demon's Souls*. PlayStation.

———. 2011. *Dark Souls*. Microsoft Windows.

———. 2014. *Dark Souls 2*. Microsoft Windows.

———. 2015. *Bloodborne*. PlayStation.

———. 2016. *Dark Souls 3*. Microsoft Windows.

———. 2019. *Sekiro: Shadows Die Twice*. Microsoft Windows.

———. 2022. *Elden Ring*. Microsoft Windows.

Genette, Gérard. 1980. *Narrative Discourse: An Essay in Method*. Translated by J. E. Lewin. Ithaca, NY: Cornell University Press.

Gert, Bernard, and Joshua Gert. 2020. "The Definition of Morality." In *The Stanford Encyclopedia of Philosophy*, edited by Edward N. Zalta. https://plato.stanford.edu/archives/fall2020/entries/morality-definition/.

Golden Glitch. 2019. *Elsinore*. Microsoft Windows.

Green, Amy M. 2021. *Longing, Ruin, and Connection in Hideo Kojima's* Death Stranding. New York: Routledge.

Grishakova, Marina, and Maria Poulaki, eds. 2019. *Narrative Complexity: Cognition, Embodiment, Evolution*. Lincoln: University of Nebraska Press.

Gumbrecht, Hans Ulrich. 2004. *Production of Presence: What Meaning Cannot Convey*. Stanford, CA: Stanford University Press.

———. 2012. *Atmosphere, Mood, Stimmung: On a Hidden Potential of Literature*. Translated by Erik Butler. Stanford, CA: Stanford University Press.

Hakemulder, Frank. 2000. *The Moral Laboratory: Experiments Examining the Effects of Reading Literature on Social Perception and Moral Self-Concept*. Amsterdam: John Benjamins.

Hampe, Beate, and Joseph E. Grady, eds. 2005. *From Perception to Meaning: Image Schemas in Cognitive Linguistics*. Berlin: De Gruyter.

Hanson, Christopher. 2018. *Game Time: Understanding Temporality in Video Games*. Bloomington: Indiana University Press.

Haraway, Donna. 2015. "Anthropocene, Capitalocene, Plantationocene, Chthulucene: Making Kin." *Environmental Humanities* 6 (1): 159–65.

———. 2016. *Staying with the Trouble: Making Kin in the Chthulucene*. Durham, NC: Duke University Press.

Hardin, Garrett. 1968. "The Tragedy of the Commons." *Science* 162 (3859): 1243–8.

Harrison, Stephen. 2021. "Fake Reddit Post Starts Serious Debate About Video Game Accessibility." *Slate*. https://slate.com/technology/2021/04/video-game-disability-law-accessibility-path-of-exile.html.

Hayles, N. Katherine. 1999. *How We Became Posthuman: Virtual Bodies in Cybernetics, Literature, and Informatics*. Chicago: University of Chicago Press.

———. 2017. *Unthought: The Power of the Cognitive Nonconscious*. Chicago: University of Chicago Press.

Herman, David. 2009. *Basic Elements of Narrative*. Chichester: Wiley-Blackwell.

Herman, Luc, and Bart Vervaeck. 2009. "Narrative Interest as Cultural Negotiation." *Narrative* 17 (1): 111–29.

Hogan, Patrick Colm. 2022. *Literature and Moral Feeling: A Cognitive Poetics of Ethics, Narrative, and Empathy*. Cambridge: Cambridge University Press.

Huizinga, Johan. 1949. *Homo Ludens: A Study of the Play-Element in Culture*. London: Routledge.

Jahn, Manfred. 1997. "Frames, Preferences, and the Reading of Third Person Narratives." *Poetics Today* 18 (4): 441–68.

Jayemanne, Darshana. 2017. *Performativity in Art, Literature, and Videogames*. Cham: Springer.

Jenkins, Henry. 2004. "Game Design as Narrative Architecture." In *First Person: New Media as Story, Performance, and Game*, edited by Noah Wardrip-Fruin and Pat Harrigan, 118–30. Cambridge, MA: MIT Press.

Juul, Jesper. 2005. *Half-Real: Video Games between Real Rules and Fictional Worlds*. Cambridge, MA: MIT Press.

———. 2019. *Handmade Pixels: Independent Video Games and the Quest for Authenticity*. Cambridge, MA: MIT Press.

Kagen, Melissa. 2017. "Walking Simulators, #GamerGate, and the Gender of Wandering." In *The Year's Work in Nerds, Wonks, and Neocons*, edited by Jonathan P. Eburne and Benjamin Schreier, 275–300. Bloomington: Indiana University Press.

Kelly, Matthew. 2016. "I Can't Take This: *Dark Souls*, Vulnerability, and the Ethics of Networks." *First Person Scholar*. http://www.firstpersonscholar.com/i-cant-take-this/.

Kelly, Michael H., and Frank C. Keil. 1985. "The More Things Change . . . : Metamorphoses and Conceptual Structure." *Cognitive Science* 9 (4): 403–16.

Kiss, Miklós, and Steven Willemsen. 2017. *Impossible Puzzle Films: A Cognitive Approach to Contemporary Complex Cinema*. Edinburgh: Edinburgh University Press.

Kłosiński, Michał. 2022. "How to Interpret Digital Games? A Hermeneutic Guide in Ten Points, With References and Bibliography." *Game Studies* 22 (2). http://gamestudies.org/2202/articles/gap_klosinski.

Kojima Productions. 2019. *Death Stranding*. Microsoft Windows.

Korthals Altes, Liesbeth. 2014. *Ethos and Narrative Interpretation: The Negotiation of Values in Narrative Fiction*. Lincoln: University of Nebraska Press.

Krzywinska, Tanya. 2008. "World Creation and Lore: *World of Warcraft* as Rich Text." In *Digital Culture, Play, and Identity: A* World of Warcraft *Reader*, edited by Hilde Corneliussen and Jill Walker Rettberg, 123–41. Cambridge: MIT Press.

Kuiken, Don, David S. Miall, and Shelley Sikora. 2004. "Forms of Self-Implication in Literary Reading." *Poetics Today* 25 (2): 171–203.

Lahdenperä, Linda. 2018. "'Live—Die—Repeat': The Time Loop as a Narrative and a Game Mechanic." *International Journal of Transmedia Literacy* 4: 137–59.

Lakoff, George, and Mark Johnson. 1980. *Metaphors We Live By*. Chicago: University of Chicago Press.

Lamarque, Peter. 2008. *The Philosophy of Literature*. Malden, MA: Wiley-Blackwell.

Lambert, Shannon. 2022. "'Shadowtime': Michelle Paver's *Dark Matter* and Ghosts of the Anthropocene." *English Text Construction* 15 (2): 138–55.

Lauro, Sarah Juliet, and Deborah Christie. 2011. "Introduction." In *Better Off Dead: The Evolution of the Zombie as Post-Human*, edited by Deborah Christie and Sarah Juliet Lauro, 1–4. New York: Fordham University Press.

Lauro, Sarah Juliet, and Karen Embry. 2008. "A Zombie Manifesto: The Nonhuman Condition in the Era of Advanced Capitalism." *Boundary 2* 35 (1): 85–108.

Lessing, Gotthold Ephraim. 1962. *Laocoon: An Essay on the Limits of Painting and Poetry*. Translated by Edward Allen McCormick. Indianapolis: Bobbs-Merrill.

Lyonne, Natasha, Leslye Headland, and Amy Poehler, dirs. 2019. *Russian Doll*. Netflix.

Mahaffey, Vicki. 2007. *Modernist Literature: Challenging Fictions*. Malden, MA: Wiley-Blackwell.

McWhertor, Michael. 2022. "Poison Swamp-Loving Sicko at It Again with *Elden Ring*." Polygon. https://www.polygon.com/22907130/elden-ring-difficulty-poison-swamps-hidetaka-miyazaki.

Meretoja, Hanna. 2018. *The Ethics of Storytelling: Narrative Hermeneutics, History, and the Possible*. Oxford: Oxford University Press.

Miall, David S., and Don Kuiken. 1994. "Foregrounding, Defamiliarization, and Affect: Response to Literary Stories." *Poetics* 22 (5): 389–407.

Milota, Megan. 2014. "From 'Compelling and Mystical' to 'Makes You Want to Commit Suicide': Quantifying the Spectrum of Online Reader Responses." *Scientific Study of Literature* 4 (2): 178–95.

Mittell, Jason. 2015. *Complex TV: The Poetics of Contemporary Television Storytelling*. New York: New York University Press.

Mobius Digital. 2019. *Outer Wilds*. Microsoft Windows.

Morton, Timothy. 2010. *The Ecological Thought*. Cambridge, MA: Harvard University Press.

Mukherjee, Ranu, and Alicia Escott. 2015. "Shadowtime." *Bureau of Linguistical Reality*. https://bureauoflinguisticalreality.com/portfolio/shadowtime/.

Murray, Janet H. 1998. *Hamlet on the Holodeck*. Cambridge, MA: MIT Press.

Murray, Soraya. 2017. *On Video Games: The Visual Politics of Race, Gender and Space*. New York: Bloomsbury.

Nitsche, Michael. 2008. *Video Game Spaces: Image, Play, and Structure in 3D Worlds*. Cambridge, MA: MIT Press.

Nolan, Cristopher, dir. 2000. *Memento*. Summit Entertainment.

Nussbaum, Martha C. 2010. *Not for Profit: Why Democracy Needs the Humanities*. Princeton, NJ: Princeton University Press.

Olsen, Bjørnar, Michael Shanks, Timothy Webmoor, and Christopher Witmore. 2012. *Archaeology: The Discipline of Things*. Berkeley: University of California Press.

Pease, Allison. 2011. "Modernism and Mass Culture." In *The Cambridge Companion to Modernism*, edited by Michael Levenson, 197–211. Cambridge: Cambridge University Press.

Phelan, James. 2007. *Experiencing Fiction: Judgments, Progressions, and the Rhetorical Theory of Narrative*. Columbus: Ohio State University Press.

———. 2017. *Somebody Telling Somebody Else: A Rhetorical Poetics of Narrative*. Columbus: Ohio State University Press.

Pick, Anat. 2011. *Creaturely Poetics: Animality and Vulnerability in Literature and Film*. New York: Columbia University Press.

Pier, John. 2017. "Complexity: A Paradigm for Narrative?" In *Emerging Vectors of Narratology*, edited by Per Krogh Hansen, John Pier, Philippe Roussin, and Wolf Schmid, 534–65. Berlin: De Gruyter.

Pope, Lucas. 2013. *Papers, Please*. Microsoft Windows.

———. 2018. *Return of the Obra Dinn*. Microsoft Windows.

Postmes, Tom, and Suzanne Brunsting. 2002. "Collective Action in the Age of the Internet: Mass Communication and Online Mobilization." *Social Science Computer Review* 20 (3): 290–301.

Przybylski, Andrew K., and Netta Weinstein. 2019. "Violent Video Game Engagement Is Not Associated with Adolescents' Aggressive Behaviour: Evidence from a Registered Report." *Royal Society Open Science* 6 (2): 171474.

Punday, Dan. 2019. *Playing at Narratology: Digital Media as Narrative Theory*. Columbus: Ohio State University Press.

Raffel, Burton. 1968. "*The Lord of the Rings* as Literature." In *Tolkien and the Critics: Essays on J. R. R. Tolkien's* The Lord of the Rings, edited by Neil David Isaacs and Rose Abdelnour Zimbardo, 218–46. Notre Dame, IN: University of Notre Dame Press.

Rittel, Horst W. J., and Melvin M. Webber. 1973. "Dilemmas in a General Theory of Planning." *Policy Sciences* 4 (2): 155–69.

Rockstar Games. 2018. *Red Dead Redemption 2*. Microsoft Windows.

Rose, Deborah Bird. 2011. *Wild Dog Dreaming: Love and Extinction*. Charlottesville: University of Virginia Press.

Ryan, Malcolm, Paul Formosa, and Rowan Tulloch. 2019. "Playing Around With Morality: Introducing the Special Issue on 'Morality Play.'" *Games and Culture* 14 (4): 299–305.

Ryan, Marie-Laure. 1991. *Possible Worlds, Artificial Intelligence, and Narrative Theory*. Bloomington: Indiana University Press.

———. 2001. "Beyond Myth and Metaphor: The Case of Narrative in Digital Media." *Game Studies* 1 (1). http://www.gamestudies.org/0101/ryan/.

———. 2006. *Avatars of Story*. Minneapolis: University of Minnesota Press.

Schniedermann, Wibke. 2023. "The Narrative Features of Involuntary Time Loops." *Narrative* 31 (3): 290–307.

Segal, Eyal. 2010. "Closure in Detective Fiction." *Poetics Today* 31 (2): 153–215.

Shklovsky, Viktor. 1965. "Art as Technique." In *Russian Formalist Criticism: Four Essays*, edited by Lee T. Lemon and Marion J. Reis, 3–24. Lincoln: University of Nebraska Press.

Sicart, Miguel. 2009. *The Ethics of Computer Games*. Cambridge, MA: MIT Press.

———. 2013. *Beyond Choices: The Design of Ethical Gameplay*. Cambridge, MA: MIT Press.

Sissa, Giulia. 2019. "Apples and Poplars, Nuts and Bulls: The Poetic Biosphere of Ovid's *Metamorphoses*." In *Antiquities Beyond Humanism*, edited by Emanuela Bianchi, Sara Brill, and Brooke Holmes, 159–86. Oxford: Oxford University Press.

Smith, Barbara Herrnstein. 2016. "What Was 'Close Reading'?: A Century of Method in Literary Studies." *Minnesota Review* 87 (1): 57–75.

Smith, Jonas Heide. 2007. "Tragedies of the Ludic Commons: Understanding Cooperation in Multiplayer Games." *Game Studies* 7 (1). http://gamestudies.org/0701/articles/smith.

Sontag, Susan. 2001. "Against Interpretation." In *Against Interpretation: And Other Essays*, 3–14. New York: Picador.

Steiner, George. 2004. "'Tragedy,' Reconsidered." *New Literary History* 35 (1): 1–15.

The Fullbright Company. 2013. *Gone Home*. Microsoft Windows.

The Game Kitchen. 2013. *The Last Door*. "The Letter" (Episode 1). Microsoft Windows.

Thon, Jan-Noël. 2014. "Toward a Transmedial Narratology: On Narrators in Contemporary Graphic Novels, Feature Films, and Computer Games." In *Beyond Classical Narration: Transmedial and Unnatural Challenges*, edited by Jan Alber and Per Krogh Hansen, 25–56. Berlin: De Gruyter.

Todorov, Tzvetan. 1968. "La Grammaire Du Récit." *Langages* 12: 94–102.

Tyson, James. 2022. "*Elden Ring*'s Grace Sure Look Like Humanity Sprites." *Screenrant*. https://screenrant.com/elden-ring-grace-dark-souls-humanity-easter-egg/.

Ueda, Fumito. 2005. *Shadow of the Colossus*. PlayStation.

Valentine, Rebekah. 2022. "*Elden Ring*'s Player Messages Are the Most Fascinating Social Media Platform of 2022." *IGN*. https://www.ign.com/articles/elden-rings-player-messages-fascinating-social-media-platform-2022.

Varela, Francisco J., Evan Thompson, and Eleanor Rosch. 1991. *The Embodied Mind: Cognitive Science and Human Experience*. Cambridge, MA: MIT Press.

Varnson, Fletcher. 2022. "How *Elden Ring*'s Sky Temple Fell to the Earth." *Screenrant*. https://screenrant.com/elden-ring-sky-temple-story-lore-farum-azula/.

Vella, Daniel. 2013. "'It's A-Me/Mario': Playing as a Ludic Character." In *Foundations of Digital Games Conference Proceedings*, 31–8. http://www.fdg2013.org/program/papers/paper05_vella.pdf.

———. 2015. "No Mastery Without Mystery: *Dark Souls* and the Ludic Sublime." *Game Studies* 15 (1). http://gamestudies.org/1501/articles/vella.

Viveiros de Castro, Eduardo. 2004. "Exchanging Perspectives: The Transformation of Objects into Subjects in Amerindian Ontologies." *Common Knowledge* 10 (3): 463–84.

Walton, Kendall. 1990. *Mimesis as Make-Believe: On the Foundations of the Representational Arts*. Cambridge, MA: Harvard University Press.

Wei, Huaxin, Jim Bizzocchi, and Tom Calvert. 2010. "Time and Space in Digital Game Storytelling." *International Journal of Computer Games Technology*. https://doi.org/10.1155/2010/897217.

Welsh, Timothy. 2020. "(Re)Mastering *Dark Souls*." *Game Studies* 20 (4). http://gamestudies.org/2004/articles/welsh#_ednref2.

Willemsen, Steven, and Miklós Kiss. 2020. "Keeping Track of Time: The Role of Spatial and Embodied Cognition in the Comprehension of Nonlinear Storyworlds." *Style* 54 (2): 172–98.

Wilson, Anthony. 2018. *Swamp: Nature and Culture*. London: Reaktion Books.

Wolfe, Cary. 2010. *What Is Posthumanism?* Minneapolis: University of Minnesota Press.

Yacobi, Tamar. 1981. "Fictional Reliability as a Communicative Problem." *Poetics Today* 2 (2): 113–26.

Young, Helen. 2015. *Race and Popular Fantasy Literature: Habits of Whiteness*. New York: Routledge.

Zoran, Gabriel. 1984. "Towards a Theory of Space in Narrative." *Poetics Today* 5 (2): 309–35.

Zunshine, Lisa. 2008. *Strange Concepts and the Stories They Make Possible: Cognition, Culture, Narrative*. Baltimore: Johns Hopkins University Press.

Index

For Product Safety Concerns and Information please contact our EU representative GPSR@taylorandfrancis.com
Taylor & Francis Verlag GmbH, Kaufingerstraße 24, 80331 München, Germany

www.ingramcontent.com/pod-product-compliance
Ingram Content Group UK Ltd.
Pitfield, Milton Keynes, MK11 3LW, UK
UKHW021055080625
459435UK00003B/15

* 9 7 8 1 0 3 2 6 8 3 9 9 7 *